The Volumetrics **Cookbook** for Jenny Craig

HarperCollins books may be purchased for educational, business, or sales promotional use. For information, please write: Special Markets Department, HarperCollins Publishers Inc., 10 East 53rd Street, New York, NY 10022.

Designed by Laura Lindgren and Jessica Shatan

Printed on acid-free paper

Library of Congress Cataloging-in-Publication Data

Rolls, Barbara J.
    The Volumetrics Cookbook for Jenny Craig : Recipes for Satisfaction and Success Based
    on Volumetrics by Barbara Rolls, Ph.D.
    p. cm.
    ISBN 0-06-112900-3
    1. Reducing diets—Recipes.   2. Appetite.   3. Food—Caloric content.   I. Title.
    RM222.2.R6275 2005   2004054045
    641.5'635—dc22

06 07 08 09 10 9 8 7 6 5 4 3

Jenny Craig®

The Volumetrics
Cookbook for
Jenny Craig

Recipes for Satisfaction and Success
Based on *Volumetrics by Barbara Rolls, PH.D.*

HarperCollins*Publishers*

Contents

Contents

Welcome to Volumetrics for Jenny Craig

Who would have guessed that one of the best strategies for weight loss success was to eat more, not less? Years of dieting might have programmed you to cut calories, reduce fat, and minimize portion size in order to reach your goal. While these tactics can be useful, they leave out one critical element: satisfaction.

At Jenny Craig, we work with an esteemed Medical Advisory Board. One member, Dr. Barbara Rolls, is renowned for her nutrition research on appetite. In her work at The Pennsylvania State University, Dr. Rolls investigates how the portion size, fat content and calorie density of different foods affect how much people eat and how hungry they feel.

Based on her research, Dr. Rolls developed "Volumetrics," a set of techniques for feeling full on fewer calories. Low calorie or high calorie, macaroni and cheese or mixed salad, people tend to eat the same amount of food at a meal. Dr. Rolls has shown that, if you can lower the calorie density of the foods in a meal, you can reduce the total calories consumed at that meal. Keep doing that, meal after meal, day after day, and you have a satisfying strategy that supports successful weight loss.

Jenny Craig clients seldom complain of hunger or feelings of deprivation. That's because satisfaction is built into the Jenny Craig menu in two ways. First, physical satisfaction is built in to the menu by emphasizing low calorie density foods like fruits, vegetables, high fiber starches and lean protein. Second, emotional satisfaction is built in to the menu by regularly featuring Jenny Craig snacks, like Chocolate Cake and Cheese Curls, in moderate portions. It's this skill of balancing lower calorie density foods you eat in abundance with higher calorie density foods you eat in moderation that is essential to healthy weight management.

The recipes in this cookbook, which are adapted from Dr. Rolls' book, *The Volumetrics Eating Plan*, offer delicious inspiration for your own Volumetrics meal planning.

Whether you are losing or maintaining your weight, you'll find *The Volumetrics Cookbook for Jenny Craig* to be a fun and informative tool for creating a healthy relationship with food.

Introducing Dr. Barbara Rolls

As a researcher, I spend my days investigating new developments in the field of nutrition that can help people to successfully manage their weight. It is an exciting field that is advancing rapidly, and I am gratified by my work every day.

As a professor of nutritional sciences at The Pennsylvania State University, I firmly believe in the need for diets that promote both weight loss and health benefits. I am passionate about sharing healthy weight loss strategies with individuals who have struggled with their weight and tried too many quick fixes or miracle cures that did not work in the past. I am also very practical and understand that people need simple, scientifically sound suggestions for balancing healthy eating with regular physical activity.

It's this combination of strong science and easy practicality that has made the principles detailed in my two books, *The Volumetrics Weight-Control Plan* and *The Volumetrics Eating Plan*, so popular, both with health care professionals and consumers. Over and over, I'm told that the visual model of Volumetrics is a simple and straightforward guide to healthy menu planning.

With its focus on health, convenience, and practical strategies for lifestyle change, Volumetrics is a natural addition to your Jenny Craig Program. Inside this customized cookbook, you'll find volumetric recipes and tips you can immediately begin to use as a part of your Jenny Craig Menu. As you progress through your Program and practice more independent planning, you can continue to make Volumetrics a part of your own menus. Once you become familiar with the strategies in this cookbook, you may even want to learn more by reading the original version, *The Volumetrics Eating Plan*.

One of the biggest challenges I have with most diets is that they focus on foods to avoid. Volumetrics, though, focuses on foods to include—and to enjoy—in satisfying amounts. This focus fits with Jenny Craig's own philosophy that the pleasure of eating is critical to a healthy eating style. Be assured that the Volumetrics strategies you'll find in this cookbook will support both your weight loss and weight maintenance efforts as they show you how to create an eating pattern that you can sustain for life.

1 Understanding Volumetrics

If you have found that your weight has been creeping up over the years, you are certainly not alone. More than half of all adults in America are overweight or obese. We are surrounded by a huge variety of tempting high-calorie foods, and we are less and less active. For most of us, it is difficult to avoid putting on weight in this obesigenic environment. To resist the almost inevitable weight gain over time, you need sound strategies. I will show you what recent research reveals about how to choose foods that will help you to maintain or reach your optimal weight.

First, let me share with you some information about why I am qualified to help direct your food choices. I have spent my career studying eating behavior and weight management. As a professor of nutritional sciences at The Pennsylvania State University, I train students and conduct research funded by the National Institutes of Health. My lab includes a large research kitchen and dining area. For our studies, people come to the dining area to eat. We test how different properties of foods such as calorie density, fat content, or portion size affect how much people eat, how hungry they feel, and what affects the enjoyment of the foods being eaten. Our studies have led to a better understanding of which foods can help curb hunger without adding extra calories. It is exciting to be doing work that has an impact on the biggest health challenge we have ever faced as a nation—the obesity epidemic.

Volumetrics is an eating plan based on the latest research on how to control hunger while managing calories to lose weight or to hold steady at your current weight. The plan also helps ensure that you are eating a balanced and nutritious diet. Often, when people decide to make the commitment to lose weight, they forget that the foods they eat affect a lot more than their weight. When you are eating fewer calories than you normally do, it is more important than ever to eat a good balance of nutrients. Because you are eating less, you are already at a higher risk of not getting an adequate amount of key nutrients. Dieting is the worst possible time to cut out entire food groups. Although Volumetrics can be used to help achieve your goal weight, it is not just for those who want to manage their weight. Since the plan is a practical guide to nutritious and satisfying foods, it will help to establish habits associated with eating well for optimal health.

Volumetrics

- Focuses on what you can eat, not on what you must give up.
- Is based on sound nutritional advice widely accepted by health professionals.
- Emphasizes that the only proven way to lose weight is to eat fewer calories than your body uses as fuel for your activities.
- Stresses that when you are managing calories it is more important than ever to eat a good balance of foods and nutrients.
- Teaches you to make food choices that will help control hunger and enhance satiety.
- Shows you how to fit your favorite foods into your diet.
- Reinforces eating and activity patterns that you can sustain for a lifetime of achieving your own healthy weight.

Both of these meals contain 500 calories. Yes, that is right; they both contain the same number of calories! The traditional meal in the top photo gives you only small portions of fried chicken, mashed potatoes, and cheesy broccoli. The large meal in the bottom photo is based on the principles of Volumetrics. This volumetric meal is reduced in fat, high in fruits and veggies, and full of flavor. Which meal would you find to be more satisfying?

CALORIE DENSITY

When trying to consume fewer calories, you should be aware of the amount of calories in a given weight of food (calories per gram). A food that is high in calorie density provides a large amount of calories in a small weight, while a food of low calorie density has fewer calories for the same amount (weight). With foods of lower calorie density, you can eat a larger portion (weight). To enhance satiety, you want to choose foods that contain the smallest number of calories in the biggest portion—these are foods low in calorie density.

Why does this matter? Research shows that, over a day or two, a person will eat about the same weight of food. Obviously, there is some variability—on days that someone eats out, for example, she may eat more food. But, in general, when scientists have looked at what people report they eat, or when food intake has been measured in the lab, the weight of food a person eats is more similar from day to day than the number of calories consumed. It seems that we have learned how much food it takes to satisfy our hunger, and that is what we choose to eat. In my lab, we have conducted a number of studies showing that people help themselves to equal amounts of similar foods regardless of the calorie content. Therefore, when the calorie density of a food, such as a casserole, is reduced by adding water or water-rich vegetables, people eat the same amount of food and, as a result, they eat fewer calories. Significantly, they feel just as full and satisfied.

The takeaway message from these studies is that by choosing foods that have fewer calories in your usual weight of food, you will end up eating fewer calories. And you won't feel any hungrier!

I am going to give you lots of tips as to how to lower the calorie density of your diet so that you can eat a satisfying amount of food while losing weight.

Adding water-rich ingredients such as vegetables lowers the calorie density. Cutting out some of the fat can also lower it. Fat is the most calorie-dense component of food. It really packs the calories into food, providing 9 calories per gram, more than twice as many as carbohydrates or protein, which provide 4 calories per gram. This high calorie density makes fat calories easy to overeat. In general, if you lower the fat content of a food, you will get a bigger portion for the same number of calories. Think about it—if you leave the butter off your bread, you can have two slices instead of one buttered slice for the same 140 calories. If you choose skim milk rather than whole milk, you will get almost twice as much for the same calories.

While fat has a big impact on calorie density, water has an even greater effect. Water has a calorie density of 0. It has weight but no calories at all! Foods with a high water content influence satiety because water dilutes the calories in food, adding weight and volume without adding calories. If you choose water-rich foods, you can have satisfying portions with few calories. Consider grapes compared to raisins. They are the same food, but removing the water drastically affects how much you can eat. In a 100-calorie snack, you get only 1/4 cup of raisins compared to 2 cups of grapes.

Where the calories are

To understand where the calories are in your food, imagine that each of the scale weights is a 1-gram weight (there are 28 grams in an ounce). Each dot represents one calorie. The number of dots shows the calorie density of the major components of the foods you eat. As you can see, the calorie density varies widely, from 9 calories per gram (cal/g) for fat, 7 for alcohol, 4 for carbohydrate and protein, 2 for fiber, to 0 for water. Remember that low-calorie-dense foods with few calories per gram give you bigger, more satisfying portions than high-calorie-dense foods.

Fat
9 cal/g

Alcohol
7 cal/g

Carbohydrate
4 cal/g

Protein
4 cal/g

Fiber
2 cal/g

Water
0 cal/g

Don't think that you can simply drink lots of water—this is healthy, but it won't fill you up. You'll need to eat more foods that are naturally rich in water, such as fruits, vegetables, low-fat milk, and cooked grains. You should also be eating more water-rich dishes: soups, stews, casseroles, pasta with vegetables, and fruit-based desserts. But you'll have to limit the portion size and frequency of foods that are low in water, such as high-fat foods like potato chips, as well as low-fat and fat-free foods that contain little moisture, like pretzels, crackers, and fat-free cookies.

The water content of foods

There are huge differences in the water content of foods. Choose foods that have high water content and you will feel full on fewer calories.

Food	Water Content (percent)
Fruits and vegetables	80–95
Soups	80–95
Hot cereal	85
Yogurt, low-fat, fruit flavored	75
Egg, boiled	75
Pasta, cooked	65
Fish and seafood	60–85
Meats	45–65
Bread	35–40
Cheese	35
Nuts	2–5
Saltine crackers	3
Potato chips	2
Oil	0

FIBER AND OTHER CARBOHYDRATES

Grains, breads, cereals, vegetables, fruits, and refined sugar contain primarily carbohydrates, which serve as the body's main fuel. This broad range of foods provides more than half of the calories most of us consume. You don't have to eliminate carbohydrates from your diet to lose weight—to do so would mean you would miss out on valuable nutrients. Instead, choose wisely—go for the carbohydrate-containing foods that provide the most nutrients and the most satiety. Choose those high in water and fiber, particularly vegetables, fruits, and whole grains.

Fiber is a form of carbohydrate that cannot be fully digested. Because it has so few calories that your body can use (1.5 to 2.5 per gram) compared to other nutrients, the addition of fiber helps to reduce the calorie density of foods. However, since only small amounts can be added to most foods, fiber's impact on calorie density is less than that of water. Fiber has been shown to increase satiety not only by lowering the calorie density of foods but also by slowing the rate that foods pass through the digestive system. Most people fall far short of the recommended fiber intake, which is 25 grams a day for women and 38 grams for men. Choosing fiber-rich foods can help you to lose weight while eating nutritious foods. Simply doubling the amount of fiber you eat from the average of 15 grams per day to around 30 grams helps reduce calorie intake. Even better for those of you wanting to lose weight is that studies have shown that, in just four months, this increased fiber intake resulted in the consumption of fewer calories, which led to an average weight loss of five pounds—with no dieting!

Generally, whole foods, rather than those that have been processed, are good choices. Processing can destroy or remove the fiber from foods so they provide less satiety. For example, whole fruit is more satiating than juice, which contains little fiber. Look for whole grains, as they are nutritious and require more chewing, which slows eating and provides lots of sensory satisfaction.

Where to find the fiber

- Always think about how you can add vegetables and fruits to meals and snacks.
- Eat fruits and vegetables whole, peeling only when necessary.
- Find the whole grains—look in breads and cereal.
  - Check the label. You are looking for breads that are 100 percent whole-wheat or grain or that list the whole grains first in the ingredients. Look for at least 2 grams of fiber per slice.
  - Choose breakfast cereals wisely. For healthy fast food in a box, find high-fiber cereals you enjoy. Select cereals that have at least 3 grams of fiber per serving.
  - Choose brown rice and whole-wheat or wheat-blend pasta.
- Look for legumes such as kidney beans or black beans, lentils, chickpeas, and split peas, which are loaded with fiber.
  - Add these to pastas, soups, and stews.

PROTEIN FOR WEIGHT LOSS

You probably have heard a lot about higher-protein, lower-carbohydrate diets and weight loss in recent years. Some people say they find it easy to stick to these diets, at least for a while. This may be because high-protein foods can decrease hunger and prolong satiety more than foods high in either carbohydrate or fat. Eating enough protein-rich foods of low calorie density is a good strategy for increasing satiety, especially if you are trying to lose weight. But eating more protein than your body needs is not going to boost your metabolism, build more muscle, or make you thinner! When you cut calories, you should make sure you are eating an adequate amount of protein and that your sources of protein are low in fat. The amount of protein you need each day is based on your body weight. The usual recommendation is 0.4 grams per pound ideal body weight. If you are very active, you can go up to 0.8 grams per pound.

FINDING FLAVOR WITH LESS FAT

Fat adds delicious textures and carries the flavors in many of our favorite foods, so trying to give up all of the fat in your diet is not a palatable long-term solution to cutting calories. Plus, some fats are healthy, such as those in fish, nuts, avocados, and olives. You need to remind yourself that decreasing the amount of fat you eat will lower the calorie density of your diet. In general, the lower the fat, the bigger the portion you get for the same number of calories. You need to find a level of fat in your food that helps you to lower the calorie density, but still gives you enjoyment.

Once you learn to identify the sources of fat in your diet, there are many simple steps you can take to eat less without sacrificing taste. Check the Nutrition Facts label on food packages, looking at the number of fat grams per serving and for fat-related packaging claims. About 20 to 30 percent of your calories should come from fat, which is 36 to 53 grams of fat per day if you are eating 1600 calories per day. An easy way to reduce your total fat intake is to eat more reduced-fat and low-fat foods and fewer high-fat foods. Foods specifically labeled low-fat have 3 grams or less of fat per serving, while those labeled reduced-fat or less fat have at least 25 percent less fat per serving than the food to which it is being compared.

Finding tasty reduced-fat foods is easier than ever before. Not only are there more products on the market than in the past, but are continually being improved, so they taste more like the full-fat foods. Make sure that you choose reduced-fat foods that are also lower in calories than their original version—check labels to compare calories. Try some of the new reduced-fat products—salad dressings are popular and even reduced-fat cheese has improved over the early rubbery versions. If you like them, use them to replace the higher fat options. This way you will be able to eat satisfying portions and keep your fat and calories under control.

While it is important to choose reduced-fat foods, you should keep in mind that not all fats are the same. Different types of fat have different effects on your health. You may have heard of monounsaturated fat, the type of fat found in fish, olives, nuts, and avocados. Monounsaturated fats, especially the omega-3 fatty acids found in fish, provide important health benefits, and may help reduce your risk of heart disease. You should enjoy moderate portions of foods containing monounsaturated fats. Remember that all fats are similar in calorie density, so all are easy to overeat.

You should avoid saturated fats and trans fats—they can raise your blood cholesterol levels and increase your risk of heart disease. Saturated fats are found in red meat and full-fat dairy products; trans fats, often referred to as partially hydrogenated oils, are found in many commercial baked goods and fried foods. Limiting your intake of saturated fats and trans fats not only helps you lower the calorie density of your diet, but can also help improve your cardiovascular health.
Obvious ways to reduce the amount of oils, high-fat spreads, dressings, and sauces in your diet are to simply eat fewer of these foods or to eat them less often.

Use these foods when it really matters to you—avoid using them out of habit. For example, if you dislike tossed salad without dressing, use only the amount of dressing necessary to give it a pleasant taste. On the other hand, if you can eat your dinner roll plain instead of simply spreading butter on it out of habit, break that habit and save those fat grams for foods that are more important to you.

Fat reduction strategies

Substitute reduced-fat or low-fat items for high-fat items
- Choose nonfat, low-fat, or reduced-fat spreads and dressings.
- Select broth-based soups rather than cream-based soups.
- Top a baked potato with nonfat or low-fat yogurt or sour cream.

Use alternative food items to flavor food when cooking
- Sauté mushrooms, onions, garlic, celery, and other veggies in bouillon, low-fat chicken stock, wine, or seasoned water instead of butter, margarine, or oil.
- Season your food with vegetables. Diced onions, garlic, celery, and bell peppers add flavor to many recipes.
- Enhance the taste of your foods with nonfat sauces and condiments such as ketchup, mustard, salsa, soy sauce, sweet-and-sour sauce, hot-pepper sauce, teriyaki sauce, fresh ginger, horseradish, vinegar, and Worcestershire sauce.
- Experiment with creative ways to add flavor to your foods without adding fat. For example, you can try lemon zest on rice, lime juice on fish, orange juice on pork, tomato salsa on baked chicken, or mustard on beef and chicken.
- Use herbs and spices.

Use alternative cooking methods
- Use cooking methods that are lower in added fat: baking, broiling, roasting, microwaving, steaming, and grilling.
- Use nonstick pans and skillets.
- Switch to cooking sprays in place of butter, margarine, or oil.
- Lightly stir-fry or sauté in small amounts of olive or canola oil or reduced-sodium broth.

BEVERAGES

What about beverages? If water-rich foods fill you up, won't drinks be even better? The answer is no. Many beverages such as soda and juice satisfy thirst, but not hunger. The calories from drinks consumed before a meal or during a meal add on to the food calories. You are unlikely to eat less just because you are drinking calories. One study in my lab found that calorie intake increased significantly when people drank a beverage containing 150 calories with lunch, compared to when they had a calorie-free beverage.

The good news is that many of you will be able to reduce your intake of calorie-laden drinks without feeling much of a sacrifice. Water is your best choice for quenching thirst, but there are lots of other low-calorie beverages. You can try diet soda or a fruit spritzer made by diluting fruit juice with seltzer. Hot or cold tea is fine, but don't load it up with sugar. Coffee on its own is virtually calorie free, but those coffeehouse mixes of coffee, sugar, and fat, such as lattes, can pack a meal's worth of calories into a single drink.

Calories from alcoholic beverages also add on to food calories. Alcohol is high in calorie density with 7 calories per gram, and it is often mixed with sugar-laden liquids such as soda or juice. I am not going to ask you to give up alcohol altogether. Drinking a glass of wine with dinner is okay, but remember that a 4-ounce glass has around 85 calories. You have to budget those calories into your plan.
So, be wise when choosing your drinks. Remind yourself that, for every 12-ounce soda you don't drink, you save 150 calories. If you saved 150 calories every day, that could mean up to a 15-pound weight loss in a year!

*Adapted from The Volumetrics Eating Plan. Copyright 2005 by Barbara Rolls, Ph.D.

2 Volumetrics for Jenny Craig

NUTRITION AT JENNY CRAIG

The Jenny Craig Program takes a comprehensive approach to weight management, focusing on three key success factors—Food, Body, and Mind. The Food component is designed to give you all the skills, strategies and information to create a personal eating style that you can enjoy for life. It is also designed to reflect the latest government guidelines and recommendations of leading health organizations for disease prevention.

The 2005 Dietary Guidelines for Americans defines a healthy diet as one that:

- Emphasizes fruits, vegetables, whole grains and reduced fat milk products
- Includes lean meats, poultry, fish, beans, eggs, and nuts
- Promotes heart healthy fats and limits saturated fats, trans fats, cholesterol, salt (sodium) and added sugars

The 2005 Guidelines are represented in a graphic, called MyPyramid, which symbolizes the need to take a personalized approach to healthy eating and physical activity.

The Jenny Craig Program shares this same philosophy in tailoring your Menu to your individual eating style and food/menu preferences. As you incorporate volumetric principles into your meal planning, know that the guidance you receive from Jenny Craig is designed to support both your weight and wellness goals.

Jenny Craig Menus Daily Calorie Levels

Weight Loss Menu	1200-2300 calories
Weight Loss Maintenance	1500-2600 calories

*All values are approximate and may vary based on food choice and calorie level

A COOKBOOK DESIGNED FOR YOU

Would you like to learn ways to add new flavor and greater variety to your Jenny Craig weight loss menu? Are you interested in applying these ideas to Meals on Your Own or Maintenance Menus? Then this cookbook is for you!

Each Recipe Features:

A nutritional analysis	A list of food group servings*	Volumizing tips

*Many of the ingredients in the recipes count as "free" foods, or foods that provide 0-30 calories per serving, so they were not calculated as food group servings and should not affect your weight loss progress.

How To Use This Cookbook

Whether your goal is weight loss or weight maintenance, you can use the recipes in this cookbook to enhance the flavor and satisfaction of your Menu.

Weekly Weight Loss Menus

See the Salads and Salad Dressings, Sides, and Desserts sections of this cookbook to experiment with the added Garden Salads, vegetables, fruits and starches listed on your weekly Planned/Personalized Menu.

Meal on My Own Menus

Refer to the Breakfast, Meatless, Beef, Fish and Shellfish and Poultry sections as a foundation for building your Meal on My Own Menus. Don't forget the Soup, Sandwich and Salads sections—all offer wonderful lunch/dinner options. Entertaining others? Browse the Appetizers section for savory suggestions that enable you to enjoy the party without indulging in extra unplanned calories. Or, if you're the invited guest, volunteer to bring something from the Desserts section—no one need know it's a low-calorie dish!

Halfway or Maintenance Menus

If you are at halfway or maintenance, all the recipes offer great meal planning ideas for everyday or special occasions with family and friends. The food group servings for many recipes fit especially well into maintenance calorie levels.

VOLUMETRIC STRATEGIES—YOUR STYLE

Jenny Craig Weight Loss Menu

From day one of your Jenny Craig Program, you can begin working volumetric strategies into your Jenny Craig Menu. As you'll see, there are a variety of ways for you to add volume and satisfaction to both your Jenny's Cuisine and added grocery foods. See the suggestions below for meal-by-meal strategies to enhance your variety and satisfaction.

At Breakfast...

Choose volumetric starches – When it comes to toast, bagels or English muffins, shop for those that are high in fiber and whole grain.

Add in free foods – Top egg dishes with salsa, toast with sugarfree jam/fruit spread and cereal or yogurt with ½ cup strawberries, cantaloupe or grapefruit from the Free Foods List in your Jenny's Grocery List. All of these foods enhance flavor for minimal calories.

At Lunch...

Volumize your Garden Salads – Veggies count as free foods on your menu, so you can double/triple/quadruple your daily portions for few calories. Also, mix fat-free dressing (also a free food) with your Jenny Craig Salad Dressing to "stretch" the wetness factor for the larger portion. See the Salad section for low calorie density ideas you can substitute for the Garden/Spinach Salads listed on your Menu. Chopped vegetables also add instant crunch to your Jenny Craig Tuna and Chicken Salads, soups and stews.

Go "light" on the added meats – If your Menu calls for an added ounce, look for lean protein choices – those that contain < 3 grams of fat per ounce. Also, remember to think of easy add-ons like cooked beans, tofu and reduced fat cottage or hard cheese.

At Dinner...

Volumize your veggies – As with salads, you can multiply your vegetable servings to your heart's content with very little effect on your total calorie intake. Just be sure to avoid increasing the fat servings listed on your menu. For extra flavor, top with herbs, lemon and saucy condiments like mustard, vinegar or salsa.

Volumize your entrees – Many of the grain/pasta-based Jenny's Cuisine can easily be combined with your favorite diced vegetables. Refresh your menu with either fresh, seasonal favorites or convenient frozen mixes that run the gamut of Asian to Italian to all-American varieties.

BUILDING YOUR MEAL ON MY OWN

Begin by identifying the foods you'd like to eat and build your meals around them, being sure to match the food group servings identified on your Meal on My Own section of the menu.

Breakfast

If you wanted to enjoy Piquant Frittata, your menu could look like this:

Meal on My Own Food Groups

1 Meat, 2 Starch, 1 Fat, 1 Milk*

*Can also count as 1 lean meat for a total of 2 meat servings at Breakfast

Menu Items	Food Groups
Piquant Frittata	2 meats, 2 vegetables (free), 1 fat
2 slices whole wheat toast	2 starches
1 tsp sugar-free jam	1 free food
½ cup strawberries	1 free food

How we lowered calorie density

- Added vegetables and egg whites
- Used reduced fat cheese
- To increase fiber, chose high fiber bread
- Traded margarine for sugar-free jam
- Added free fruit (strawberries)

Lunch

Plan your lunch to give you energy to last the afternoon. How about partnering the Mediterranean Turkey Sandwich on page 60 with a Garden Salad with Fat-Free Dressing?

Meal on My Own Food Groups
2 Meats, 2 Starches, 1 Vegetable and 1 Fat

Menu Items	Food Groups
Mediterranean Sandwich	2 meats, 2 starches, 1 vegetable, 1 fat
Garden Salad with Fat-Free Italian Dressing	1 vegetable (free), 1 free food
Iced Tea with Lemon	1 free food

How we lowered calorie density
- Added vegetables to increase the volume of the sandwich
- Used lean protein on the sandwich
- Selected a high fiber bread
- Added a salad with fat-free dressing
- Made a sugar-free beverage choice

Dinner

Start with your entrée, then think of ways to include extra veggies and whole grains. Or, build your meal on starches and veggies and accent with lean meat or meat substitutes. Perhaps Chicken Merlot over a bed of 1 cup steamed brown rice with Insalata Mista would be nice?

Meal on My Own Food Groups
4 Meats, 2 Starches, 1 Vegetable and 1 Fat

Menu Items	Food Groups
Chicken Merlot	3 meats, 2 vegetables (free)
1 cup brown rice	2 starches
Insalata Mista	1 vegetable, 1 fat
2 Tbls shredded Parmesan	1 meat
Sparkling Water with Lemon	1 free food

How we lowered calorie density
* Used skinless, white chicken
* Used less oil
* Add more veggies (free)
* Used Canadian bacon instead of regular bacon

REMEMBER YOUR FREE FOODS LIST

You can enjoy unlimited amounts of non-starchy vegetables, such as tomatoes, cucumbers, onions and mushrooms for variety and satisfaction. You can also enjoy calorie-free beverages, sugar substitutes, flavor enhancers such as herbs and spices, sugar-free gelatin dessert and sugar-free gum. Other foods, such as whipped topping or sugar-free syrup and some fat-free condiments are recommended in limited amounts, up to three servings a day on your menu. See the Free Foods List below for ideas.

FREE FOODS: (0-30 calories per serving)

Unlimited

• **Free Beverages:** Coffee, Tea, Diet Soda, Diet Tonic, Club Soda, Carbonated or Mineral Water, Sugar-Free Drink Mixes (0 calories). If you choose to decrease your caffeine intake, do so gradually.

• **Sugar Substitutes:** Equal,® Splenda,® Sweet'N Low,® Sweet One® (0 calories)

• **Gelatin Dessert, Sugar-Free** (0-10 calories)

• **Gum, Sugar-Free** (0-10 calories)

• **Flavor Enhancers:** Bouillon/Broth (low-sodium), Ketchup, Extracts, Garlic, Herbs (fresh or dried), Horseradish, Lemon Juice, Lime Juice, Mustard, Pickles, Pimiento, Salsa, Spices, Soy Sauce (light), Taco Sauce, Vinegar, Worcestershire Sauce (0-25 calories).

• **Non-Starchy Vegetables:** Artichoke, Asparagus, Beans (green, wax, Italian), Bean Sprouts, Beets, Broccoli, Brussels Sprouts, Cabbage, Carrots, Cauliflower, Celery, Cucumber, Eggplant, Greens (collard, kale, mustard, turnip), Jicama, Leeks, Mushrooms, Okra, Onions, Pea Pods, Peppers (all varieties), Radishes, Salad Greens (endive, escarole, lettuce, romaine, spinach), Sauerkraut, Summer Squash (crookneck, yellow), Tomatoes/tomato paste/tomato sauce, Turnips, Vegetable Juice (low-sodium), Water Chestnuts, Zucchini (10-25 calories).

Limited (May choose up to 3 servings/day)

• **Whipped Topping or Syrup, Sugar-Free, 1 Tbl** (10-25 calories)

• **Candy, Sugar-Free, 1 piece** (10-20 calories)

• **Fat-Free Condiments, 1 Tbl:** Cocoa Powder, Cream Cheese, Jelly (low-sugar), Margarine, Mayonnaise, Non-Dairy Creamer, Salad Dressing, Sour Cream (10-30 calories)

• **Fruits, 1/2 cup:** Cantaloupe, Strawberries, Watermelon, Grapefruit (20-30 calories)

Note: Your actual calorie level may vary based on your food selections and number of "free food" choices.

3 Breakfast

Dr. Rolls' Top Volumetrics Tips

1. Be sure to eat breakfast every day – regular breakfast eaters have a lower weight than those who skip the morning meal.
2. Plan ahead: If you skip breakfast you may end up eating more later in the day.
3. Breakfast is a great time to add more whole grains to your menu, which can help reduce your risk for diabetes and heart disease.

Jennifer's Fruit-Smothered Whole-Wheat Buttermilk Pancakes, page 24

Jennifer's Fruit-Smothered Whole-Wheat Buttermilk Pancakes

Here is a great way for kids to get fruit and fiber. These fresh-fruit-and-raspberry-sauce-topped pancakes are a favorite of my lab manager's son.

1¼ cups whole-wheat flour
1½ cups low-fat buttermilk
1 beaten egg
1 tablespoon sugar
1 teaspoon baking powder

½ teaspoon baking soda
¼ teaspoon salt
½ cup Raspberry Sauce
2 cups mixed fresh blueberries,
　raspberries, and blackberries

For a 270-calorie breakfast

TRADITIONAL	How we lowered calorie density	VOLUMETRICS
Pancakes with syrup and butter	‣ Used whole-wheat flour ‣ Omitted oil and butter ‣ Replaced syrup with raspberry sauce ‣ Added fresh fruit	Jennifer's Fruit-Smothered Whole-Wheat Buttermilk Pancakes

1. In a medium mixing bowl, combine the flour, buttermilk, egg, sugar, baking powder, baking soda, and salt. Stir gently until all ingredients are mixed. The batter should be slightly lumpy.

2. Heat a skillet lightly coated with cooking spray over medium heat. Pour ¼ cup batter into the skillet for each pancake. The pancakes will be ready to flip when small bubbles appear along the sides of the pancakes. Flip and cook until the undersides are lightly browned.

3. Place 2 pancakes on each of 4 plates. Spoon 2 tablespoons raspberry sauce over the pancakes and top with ½ cup mixed berries.

YIELD: 4 servings

COOK'S NOTE: Cooked pancakes may be kept warm in a 200 degree oven while you finish cooking the rest. Other frozen berries can be substituted for the raspberries. To produce a clearer sauce and eliminate the seeds, force the raspberry mixture through a fine sieve into a bowl. The sauce provides 8 servings of 2 tablespoons each.

Nutritional Information Per Serving

Calories 270 | Carbohydrate 44 g. | Fat 3 g. | Protein 10 g. | Fiber 8 g.

Raspberry Sauce

1½ cups unsweetened frozen raspberries, thawed
2 tablespoons sugar
½ teaspoon orange liqueur or 1 tablespoon orange juice

Puree the raspberries, sugar, and liqueur in a food processor or blender. Set the Raspberry Sauce aside.

Piquant Frittata

Try this egg dish for breakfast along with fresh fruit or have it for lunch with a side salad.

5 whole eggs

7 egg whites

½ teaspoon salt

Freshly ground black pepper

1 cup nonfat shredded mozzarella cheese

1 cup chopped onions

1½ cups sliced mushrooms, about 6 ounces

1 cup diced zucchini

¾ cup chopped bottled roasted red peppers, drained

1 teaspoon dried thyme

3 tablespoons grated Parmesan cheese

For a 175-calorie entrée

TRADITIONAL	How we lowered calorie density	VOLUMETRICS
Frittata with eggs and meat	▸ Reduced number of egg yolks and cheese ▸ Used reduced-fat cheese ▸ Added more vegetables and egg whites ▸ Omitted the meat	Piquant Frittata

1. In a medium bowl, combine the eggs, egg whites, ¼ teaspoon salt, and a few grindings of black pepper and stir in the mozzarella.

2. Lightly coat a large, oven-safe, nonstick skillet with cooking spray and warm over medium heat. Add the onions and mushrooms and cook, stirring, 5 minutes. Add the zucchini, red peppers, thyme, ¼ teaspoon salt, and pinch black pepper. Cook the mixture, stirring, 4 minutes.

3. Pour the egg mixture over the vegetables and cook over medium-high heat for 7 minutes. As the eggs begin to set, run a spatula around the edges and tilt the skillet to allow any uncooked egg to run under the cooked portions. Do not stir. When the eggs are almost set, cover, reduce the heat to medium-low, and cook for 8 to 10 minutes, or until the eggs are set.

4. Preheat the broiler.

5. Sprinkle Parmesan on top of the eggs. Broil the frittata for 4 minutes or until the Parmesan is lightly browned. Cut the frittata into 6 wedges.

YIELD: 6 servings

COOK'S NOTE: Vegetables such as asparagus, broccoli, cauliflower, or yellow summer squash can be substituted for the zucchini.

Nutritional Information Per Serving

Calories 175 | Carbohydrate 9 g. | Fat 8 g. | Protein 16 g. | Fiber 1 g.

Creamy Apricot Oatmeal

This high-fiber cereal makes a hearty and satisfying breakfast.

1½ cups quick-cooking rolled oats
4 cups nonfat milk
½ teaspoon grated nutmeg
4 tablespoons oat bran

10 finely chopped dried apricots,
about 2 ounces
2 tablespoons brown sugar

1. Combine the oats and 3 cups milk in a medium saucepan. Bring the mixture to a boil over medium-high heat, stirring. Mix in the nutmeg and oat bran. Reduce the heat to low and simmer, stirring frequently, until the oats are tender, about 1 minute.

2. Divide the oatmeal among 4 cereal bowls. Sprinkle each with the apricots and brown sugar.

3. Serve the oatmeal immediately, with the remaining milk to add to the oatmeal, if desired.

YIELD: 4 servings

COOK'S NOTE: The apricots can be easily chopped using kitchen scissors. Try other dried fruit, such as dried plums, in place of the apricots. The remaining 1 cup milk can be warmed prior to serving.

Nutritional Information Per Serving

Calories 265 | Carbohydrate 47 g. | Fat 3 g. | Protein 15 g. | Fiber 5 g.

Blueberry Applesauce Muffins

These fruit-filled muffins work well for breakfast or as a snack. Applesauce replaces most of the fat traditionally used in baking, and helps keep the muffins moist.

1¾ cups all-purpose flour	1 teaspoon ground cinnamon
¾ cup light brown sugar	1¼ cups low-fat buttermilk
½ cup whole-wheat flour	1¼ cups unsweetened applesauce
2 teaspoons baking powder	1 egg
1 teaspoon baking soda	1 teaspoon vegetable oil
¼ teaspoon salt	1 teaspoon vanilla extract
¼ teaspoon grated nutmeg	1½ cups fresh blueberries

1. Preheat the oven to 400 degrees.

2. Lightly coat a 16-cup muffin pan with cooking spray.

3. Mix together 1½ cups all-purpose flour, sugar, whole-wheat flour, baking powder, baking soda, salt, nutmeg, and cinnamon in a large bowl. Make a well in the center of the mixture.

4. Whisk together the buttermilk, applesauce, egg, oil, and vanilla extract in a small bowl.

5. Toss the blueberries in ¼ cup all-purpose flour to lightly coat the berries.

6. Pour the buttermilk mixture into the flour mixture and stir until the batter is just moistened. Fold in the blueberries.

7. Divide the mixture evenly among the muffin cups. Bake the muffins for 20 minutes. Cool the muffins in the pan on a rack for 5 minutes. Remove the muffins and serve warm or at room temperature.

YIELD: 16 servings

COOK'S NOTE: Be sure to use fresh berries, as frozen may make the batter too watery.

Nutritional Information Per Serving

Calories 125 | Carbohydrate 25 g. | Fat 1 g. | Protein 3 g. | Fiber 1 g.

4 Appetizers, Starters, and Snacks

Dr. Rolls' Top Volumetrics Tips

1. Don't arrive at social events too hungry. Have a filling snack of fresh fruits or vegetables or a glass of milk before you leave home.
2. Bring a volumetric appetizer so you will be sure to have a healthy, low-calorie food to enjoy.
3. Survey the buffet and choose one plate with small servings of the foods you want to enjoy and plenty of fruits and vegetables. Avoid continuous nibbling which makes it easy to overeat.

Vegetable Party Platter, page 32

Vegetable Party Platter

Serve this colorful selection of low-calorie-dense veggies when you entertain to ensure that you and your guests will have delicious and nutritious nibbles.

2 medium cucumbers, approximately
   1 pound
2 yellow squash, about 1 pound
2 large red bell peppers, about 1 pound
2 large yellow bell peppers, about 1 pound
4 celery stalks
1 pound peeled carrots
1 pound thin asparagus

1 pint small white mushrooms, trimmed
1 pint cherry tomatoes
3 cups broccoli florets
3 cups cauliflowerettes
House Dressing (page 34)
Mel's Fresh Lemon Hummus
   (page 35)
Tex-Mex Salsa (page 36)

1. Cut the cucumbers, squash, bell peppers, celery, and carrots into ¾"-wide x 3-inch-long strips. Trim the asparagus spears and blanch them in boiling water for 4 minutes. Drain, plunge them into ice water for a few minutes, then drain again.

2. Arrange the vegetables on a large platter, placing vegetables of different colors next to each other. Place the house dressing, hummus, and salsa in serving bowls.

YIELD: 16 servings

Nutritional Information Per Serving

Calories 175 | Carbohydrate 30 g. | Fat 4 g. | Protein 10 g. | Fiber 8 g.

For a 175-calorie appetizer

TRADITIONAL	How we lowered calorie density	VOLUMETRICS
Chips and dip	▸ Replaced potato chips with vegetables ▸ Substituted low-fat dips for high-fat dips	Vegetable Party Platter

House Dressing

Coriander and cumin give this creamy salad dressing an exotic taste. It is also good as a dip with cut-up fresh vegetables.

½ teaspoon minced garlic

¼ teaspoon salt

2 tablespoons lime juice

½ teaspoon Worcestershire sauce

½ teaspoon ground coriander

½ teaspoon ground cumin

1 tablespoon minced scallions

1 cup Yogurt Cheese (page 121)

1 cup low-fat buttermilk

Pinch freshly ground black pepper

1. Whisk all the ingredients in a large bowl until blended, but still slightly chunky.

YIELD: 24 servings of 2 tablespoons each

Nutritional Information Per Serving

Calories 35 | Carbohydrate 4 g. | Fat 1 g. | Protein 3 g. | Fiber 0 g.

Mel's Fresh Lemon Hummus

This tangy hummus, developed by my daughter Melissa, is delicious either as a dip with raw vegetables or as a sandwich filling.

¼ to ⅓ cup freshly squeezed lemon juice

2 cups canned chickpeas, rinsed and
   drained

¼ cup tahini

2 teaspoons chopped garlic

1 teaspoon grated lemon zest

½ teaspoon salt

1. Puree ¼ cup lemon juice with the rest of the ingredients in a blender or food processor until the texture is slightly chunky. Taste and, if desired, stir in more lemon juice.

YIELD: 10 servings of 2 tablespoons each

Nutritional Information Per Serving

Calories 90 | Carbohydrate 13 g. | Fat 3 g. | Protein 3 g. | Fiber 2 g.

Tex-Mex Salsa

Add a Southwestern flair to any meal by using this mild salsa as a garnish for fish or chicken. It can also be used as a topping for baked potatoes or as a dip with raw vegetables.

1¾ cups canned black beans, rinsed and drained
2 cups canned whole-kernel corn, drained
1 cup seeded, chopped red or green bell peppers
½ cup chopped fresh cilantro or fresh flat-leaf parsley

1 cup chopped scallions
3 tablespoons lime juice
2 tablespoons red-wine vinegar
½ teaspoon ground cumin
¼ teaspoon salt
¼ teaspoon hot-pepper sauce

1. Combine all the ingredients in a large bowl. The salsa can be refrigerated for up to 3 days.

YIELD: 8 servings of ½ cup each

COOK'S NOTE: The flavor of this salsa intensifies as the beans and vegetables marinate.

Nutritional Information Per Serving

Calories 95 | Carbohydrate 18 g. | Fat 1 g. | Protein 5 g. | Fiber 5 g.

White Bean Bruschetta

Bruschetta (pronounced brew-sketta) is an easy to make appetizer. Just spread a tasty topping on slices of toasted or grilled bread.

*2 cups canned cannellini beans,
  rinsed and drained*
1 tablespoon lemon juice
1 tablespoon extra-virgin olive oil
1 teaspoon minced garlic
*1 tablespoon chopped, fresh flat-leaf
  parsley*

1 tablespoon chopped dill
¼ teaspoon salt
*16 slices toasted or grilled baguette,
  cut ¼-inch thick on the diagonal*
1 garlic clove, cut in half

1. Puree all ingredients except the baguette and the halved garlic clove.

2. Rub both sides of the toasted baguette slices with the cut side of the garlic halves.

3. Spread the bean mixture on the bread slices and serve.

YIELD: 16 servings of 1 toast slice and 1½ tablespoons of bean mixture each

COOK'S NOTE: For another easy topping, combine ¼ cup chopped basil with 2 cups chopped tomatoes, 1 teaspoon minced garlic, 2 teaspoons extra-virgin olive oil, ½ teaspoon salt, and a dash of pepper. Each serving has 45 calories and a calorie density of 1.2.

Nutritional Information Per Serving

Calories 60 | Carbohydrate 11 g. | Fat 1 g. | Protein 3 g. | Fiber 2 g.

Stuffed Mushrooms Florentine

These appetizers are low in calories and fat yet packed with flavor. Present them with other appetizers such as the Vegetable Party Platter (page 32) at your next party.

12 large white mushrooms, about 1½ inches across
1 teaspoon vegetable oil
¾ cup minced onions
½ teaspoon minced garlic
½ cup finely chopped spinach

½ cup seeded finely chopped red or green bell peppers
1 tablespoon fresh thyme
¼ teaspoon salt
Pinch freshly ground black pepper
1 tablespoon grated Parmesan cheese

For a 45-calorie appetizer

TRADITIONAL	How we lowered calorie density	VOLUMETRICS
Sausage-stuffed mushrooms	‣ Omitted sausage ‣ Added vegetables ‣ Decreased cheese	Stuffed Mushrooms Florentine

1. Remove, trim, and finely chop the mushroom stems, set aside.

2. Bring a medium pot of water to a boil. Blanch the mushroom caps for 2 minutes. Remove the caps and place gill side down on paper towels to drain.

3. Lightly coat a medium nonstick skillet with cooking spray, add the oil, and place over medium heat until hot. Add the reserved mushroom stems and the rest of the ingredients except the cheese, and cook, stirring occasionally, for 6 minutes. Remove the skillet from the heat and cool slightly.

4. Preheat the broiler.

5. Spoon the mixture into the mushroom caps and place on a baking sheet. Sprinkle with Parmesan. Broil the mushroom caps until light brown, about 3 minutes.

YIELD: 4 servings of 3 mushroom caps each

COOK'S NOTE: This appetizer may be frozen before broiling. When ready to proceed, thaw the mushrooms and broil as directed.

Nutritional Information Per Serving

Calories 45 | Carbohydrate 5 g. | Fat 3 g. | Protein 3 g. | Fiber 2 g.

5 Soups

Dr. Rolls' Top Volumetrics Tips

1. Start your meal with a low-calorie-dense soup. By increasing the volume by adding water or water rich ingredients, you will feel fuller and eat less of the main course.
2. If you make soup your meal, add lean meats or beans along with the veggies and broth to ensure you get a good variety of nutrients and feel satiated.
3. Make large batches of soup and freeze in single servings you can microwave later.

Hearty Chicken and Vegetable Soup, page 50

Autumn Harvest Pumpkin Soup

Start a meal with this low-fat, beautifully colored soup enlivened with cumin.

2 teaspoons unsalted butter
2 cups chopped onions
2 teaspoons all-purpose flour
4 cups nonfat, reduced-sodium chicken
  broth
3 cups plain pumpkin purée

½ teaspoon minced garlic
½ teaspoon ground cumin
¼ teaspoon salt
¼ teaspoon ground white pepper
4 tablespoons nonfat plain yogurt
Dusting of grated nutmeg

For a 150-calorie soup

TRADITIONAL	How we lowered calorie density	VOLUMETRICS
Pumpkin soup with cream, butter, and sour cream	▸ Substituted broth for cream, and yogurt for sour cream ▸ Decreased butter	Autumn Harvest Pumpkin Soup

1. Lightly coat a 4- to 5-quart nonstick saucepan or pot with cooking spray. Add the butter and place over medium heat. Add the onions and cook, stirring occasionally, 5 minutes.

2. Sprinkle in the flour and cook, stirring, 2 minutes, or until the mixture thickens slightly. Add the broth, whisking, then the pumpkin, garlic, cumin, salt, and pepper. Bring the soup to a simmer, whisking occasionally, and cook 15 minutes, stirring occasionally to prevent scorching.

3. Ladle the soup into 4 soup bowls and top with the yogurt and nutmeg.

YIELD: 4 servings of ⅔ cup each

COOK'S NOTE: Ground coriander can be substituted for cumin. Try adding a teaspoon of grated fresh ginger for extra zip. This can become a vegetarian soup by substituting 2 cups vegetable broth and 2 cups water for the chicken broth.

Nutritional Information Per Serving

Calories 150 | Carbohydrate 26 g. | Fat 3 g. | Protein 8 g. | Fiber 7 g.

Creamy Broccoli Soup

2 tablespoons unsalted butter

¾ cup chopped onions

2 tablespoons all-purpose flour

1 teaspoon dry mustard

½ teaspoon dried tarragon

Pinch ground white pepper

2 cups nonfat milk

2 cups nonfat, reduced-sodium chicken broth

4 cups chopped broccoli florets

For a 160-calorie soup

TRADITIONAL	How we lowered calorie density	VOLUMETRICS
Broccoli cheese soup	▸ Omitted cheese ▸ Used nonfat milk and chicken broth and less butter ▸ Added more broccoli	Creamy Broccoli Soup

1. Heat the butter in a 4- to 5-quart nonstick pot over medium heat. Add the onions and cook, stirring occasionally, 5 minutes.

2. Raise the heat to medium-high and stir in the flour, mustard, tarragon, and pepper and cook 2 minutes. Reduce the heat to medium. Add the milk and broth and cook, stirring frequently, 8 minutes.

3. Add the broccoli and simmer 6 minutes, stirring frequently. Remove from the heat.

4. Puree 2 cups of soup in a blender or food processor and return to the pot. Reheat, stirring occasionally, about 2 minutes.

YIELD: 4 servings of 1 cup each

COOK'S NOTE: To create a vegetarian version, substitute 1 cup vegetable broth and 1 cup water for the chicken broth.

Nutritional Information Per Serving

Calories 160 | Carbohydrate 15 g. | Fat 8 g. | Protein 9 g. | Fiber 2 g.

Rustic Tomato Soup

This Tuscan country soup provides you with a delicious way to use day-old crusty bread.

1 teaspoon extra-virgin olive oil
½ cup chopped onions
½ teaspoon chopped garlic
1½ cups canned diced tomatoes,
*   with liquid*
½ teaspoon dried oregano
¼ teaspoon salt

1½ cups nonfat, reduced-sodium chicken
*   broth*
Pinch freshly ground black pepper
4 toasted or grilled baguette slices, cut
*   ¼-inch thick on the diagonal*
Parmesan cheese shavings

1. Lightly coat a 4- to 5-quart pot with cooking spray. Add the oil and place over medium heat. Stir in the onions and garlic and cook 5 minutes, stirring often. Stir in the tomatoes, oregano, salt, and broth. Bring the soup to a simmer and cook uncovered, 20 minutes, stirring occasionally. Remove from the heat and stir in the pepper.

2. Place 1 slice of toasted bread in the bottom of each of 4 wide, shallow soup bowls. Ladle the soup over the bread. Top with a few shavings of Parmesan.

YIELD: 4 servings of 1½ cups each

COOK'S NOTE: When available, fresh basil makes a delicious addition to the soup. Stir in ½ cup chopped basil with the pepper. Tuscans traditionally use fresh vine-ripened tomatoes for this soup. For a vegetarian version, substitute 1 cup vegetable broth and ½ cup water for the chicken broth.

Nutritional Information Per Serving

Calories 125 | Carbohydrate 20 g. | Fat 3 g. | Protein 5 g. | Fiber 3 g.

Vegetarian Barley Soup

Barley provides interesting texture, a nutlike flavor, and lots of nutrients. Serve this soup as part of lunch or dinner.

½ cup chopped onions

¼ cup chopped celery

1 tablespoon chopped fresh flat-leaf parsley

½ teaspoon chopped garlic

3½ cups vegetable broth

1½ cups canned diced tomatoes, with liquid

½ cup peeled, sliced carrots

¼ cup pearl barley

¼ teaspoon salt

Pinch freshly ground black pepper

¼ teaspoon dried oregano

¼ teaspoon dried thyme

1 bay leaf

2 cups chopped mushrooms, about 6 ounces

1. Coat the bottom of a large Dutch oven or pot with cooking spray and place over medium-high heat until hot. Add the onions, celery, parsley, and garlic and cook, stirring frequently, 4 minutes.

2. Add the broth, tomatoes, carrots, barley, salt, pepper, oregano, thyme, and bay leaf and bring to a simmer, stirring occasionally. Cover the pot and simmer 20 minutes, stirring occasionally.

3. Stir in the mushrooms and simmer, uncovered, 20 minutes, stirring occasionally.

4. Remove and discard the bay leaf. Ladle the soup into 4 bowls.

YIELD: 4 servings of 1¼ cups each

COOK'S NOTE: Try different types of mushrooms to vary the flavor.

Nutritional Information Per Serving

Calories 120 | Carbohydrate 19 g. | Fat 2 g. | Protein 8 g. | Fiber 4 g.

Minestrone

Pair this vegetarian soup with a sandwich for lunch.

2 teaspoons extra-virgin olive oil
1 cup chopped onions
1 cup peeled, shredded carrots
1½ cups low-sodium vegetable juice
3 cups vegetable broth
1¼ cups cored, diced tomatoes
¾ teaspoon dried thyme
1 teaspoon dried oregano

Freshly ground black pepper
3 ounces (¾ cup) dry, whole-wheat small
   pasta shells, or other whole-wheat small
   pasta shapes
1 cup canned cannellini beans, rinsed and
   drained
3 cups shredded fresh spinach

For a 125-calorie soup

TRADITIONAL	How we lowered calorie density	VOLUMETRICS
Cream-based vegetable soup	▸ Decreased oil ▸ Omitted cream ▸ Added more veggies	Minestrone

1. Heat the oil in a 4- to 5-quart pan over medium heat. Add the onions and carrots and cook 5 minutes, stirring occasionally.

2. Add 1 cup water, vegetable juice, broth, tomatoes, thyme, oregano, and a few grindings of pepper. Bring the soup to a boil, reduce the heat, and simmer, covered, 30 minutes.

3. Prepare the pasta according to package directions.

4. Add the cooked pasta, beans, and spinach and cook over medium-low heat for 10 minutes.

YIELD: 8 servings of 1 cup each

COOK'S NOTE: For additional flavor and texture, try adding one of the following: 2 cups shredded cabbage, 2 cups sliced mushrooms, or 1 cup shredded zucchini when adding the spinach.

Nutritional Information Per Serving

Calories 125 | Carbohydrate 23 g. | Fat 2 g. | Protein 6 g. | Fiber 4.5 g.

Hearty Chicken and Vegetable Soup

Whole-wheat pasta adds fiber to this satisfying main dish soup.

2 tablespoons all-purpose flour
½ teaspoon salt
½ teaspoon dried tarragon
3 skinless, boneless chicken breast halves,
  4 to 6 ounces each, cut into 1/2-inch
    pieces
2 teaspoons vegetable oil
3 cups peeled, chopped carrots

3 cups quartered, small mushrooms,
  about ½ pound
4 cups nonfat, reduced-sodium chicken
  broth
1 teaspoon hot-pepper sauce
4 ounces dry, whole-wheat chiocciole or
  other small whole-wheat pasta
¼ cup chopped fresh flat-leaf parsley

1. Combine the flour, salt, and tarragon in a large bowl. Add the chicken and toss to coat.

2. Lightly coat the bottom of a 4- to 5-quart pot with cooking spray. Add the oil and place over medium-high heat. Add the chicken and cook, stirring frequently, 5 minutes, or until lightly browned and no longer pink inside. Remove the chicken and set aside.

3. Stir in the carrots, mushrooms, broth, and hot-pepper sauce and bring to a simmer. Cover and simmer 15 minutes, stirring occasionally.

4. Stir in the chiocciole and reserved chicken and cook 12 minutes. Ladle into 4 soup bowls and sprinkle with parsley.

YIELD: 4 servings of 2 cups each

COOK'S NOTE: Two cups of boiled brown rice may be substituted for the pasta. Stir in the rice with the chicken in step 4, cook 5 minutes, and serve as directed above.

Nutritional Information Per Serving

Calories 290 | Carbohydrate 37 g. | Fat 7 g. | Protein 24 g. | Fiber 5 g.

For a 290-calorie soup

TRADITIONAL	How we lowered calorie density	VOLUMETRICS
Chicken and vegetable soup	▸ Used lean, white chicken meat ▸ Decreased oil and pasta ▸ Increased the amount of veggies	Hearty Chicken and Vegetable Soup

6 Sandwiches and Wraps

Dr. Rolls' Top Volumetrics Tips

1. Build your sandwich with thinly sliced whole grain bread.
2. Substitute reduced-fat versions of your favorite spread or use spicy mustard.
3. Add flavor by using strong tasting vegetables such as onions, bell peppers, hot peppers, relishes, horseradish, or pickles

Zesty Tuna Salad Pita, page 58

Almond Chicken Salad Sandwich

This savory sandwich filling features the delicious combination of grapes and chicken. You can also serve the chicken salad alone on a bed of lettuce without the bread.

1½ cups diced, cooked chicken breast, about 1½ 5-ounce skinless, boneless chicken breast halves (see *Cook's Note*)

1 cup halved, seedless red grapes

¼ cup diced celery

¼ cup reduced-fat mayonnaise

1 tablespoon toasted slivered almonds

½ teaspoon freshly ground pepper

8 thin slices multigrain bread

2 cups shredded green-leaf lettuce

1. Combine the chicken, grapes, celery, mayonnaise, almonds, and pepper together in a medium bowl and mix salad well.

2. Divide the chicken salad evenly on 4 slices of the bread. Top each with ½ cup lettuce and another slice of bread.

YIELD: 4 servings

COOK'S NOTE: If you do not have cooked chicken breast meat, try this easy method. Arrange skinless, boneless chicken breasts in a saucepan. Add enough cold water to cover the chicken. Bring the water to a simmer over low heat. Turn the chicken over, cover, and remove the pan from the heat. Let the chicken sit in the pan for 15 to 20 minutes, or until it is no longer pink in the center. Remove the chicken and refrigerate until ready to use. To toast seeds or nuts, place in a skillet, and cook over moderate heat, stirring, until golden.

Nutritional Information Per Serving

Calories 275 | Carbohydrate 35 g. | Fat 6 g. | Protein 18 g. | Fiber 2 g.

Nutritional Information Per Serving of Chicken Salad

Calories 150 | Carbohydrate 10 g. | Fat 6 g. | Protein 13 g. | Fiber 1 g.

For a 275-calorie sandwich

TRADITIONAL	How we lowered calorie density	VOLUMETRICS
Chicken salad croissant	▸ Used whole-wheat bread and reduced-fat mayonnaise ▸ Added grapes	Almond Chicken Salad Sandwich

Buffalo Chicken Wraps

Try these wraps instead of fried chicken wings. The baked chicken paired with hot-pepper sauce and a low-fat blue cheese dressing gives you that comfort-food taste.

2 cups shredded, cooked chicken breast meat (See Cook's Note, Page 54)
2 tablespoons hot-pepper sauce
½ cup reduced-fat blue cheese dressing
4 10" wheat tortillas

2 cups shredded romaine lettuce
1 cup diced celery
1 cup peeled, seeded, and diced cucumber
1 cup peeled, shredded carrots

1. Combine the chicken and hot-pepper sauce in a small bowl.

2. Spread 2 tablespoons of blue cheese dressing over each tortilla. Arrange ½ cup romaine horizontally down the center of each tortilla. Top each with ½ cup chicken, ¼ cup celery, ¼ cup cucumber, and ¼ cup carrots.

3. Fold the sides of each tortilla toward the center. Starting from the bottom, tightly roll the tortilla up to the top.

YIELD: 4 servings

COOK'S NOTE: Try using flavored tortillas to add color and extra flavor.

Nutritional Information Per Serving

Calories 350 | Carbohydrate 45 g. | Fat 7 g. | Protein 28 g. | Fiber 4 g.

For a 350-calorie wrap

TRADITIONAL	How we lowered calorie density	VOLUMETRICS
Fried chicken wrap	▸ Used baked chicken instead of fried ▸ Used reduced-fat blue cheese dressing ▸ Added more veggies	Buffalo Chicken Wrap

Zesty Tuna Salad Pita

Dijon mustard sparks the flavor of this salad, and the vegetables add crunch.

2 tablespoons Dijon mustard
2 tablespoons reduced-fat mayonnaise
½ cup chopped red onions
½ cup seeded, chopped red bell peppers
½ cup seeded, chopped yellow bell peppers
½ cup chopped celery

1 12-ounce can solid white tuna packed in
    water, drained and flaked
Pinch freshly ground black pepper
4 6-inch whole-wheat pita pockets
½ cup shredded arugula or spinach
½ cup sliced mushrooms, about 1⅓ ounces

For a 285-calorie pita

TRADITIONAL	How we lowered calorie density	VOLUMETRICS
Tuna salad pita	▸ Used tuna packed in water and reduced-fat mayo ▸ Added more vegetables	Zesty Tuna Salad Pita

1. Whisk the mustard and mayonnaise in a medium bowl.

2. Add the onions, bell peppers, celery, tuna, and black pepper. Stir the tuna salad until well mixed; set aside.

3. Cut the pitas in half crosswise.

4. Divide the arugula, mushrooms, and tuna salad among the pita halves.

YIELD: 4 servings

COOK'S NOTE: You can combine the arugula, mushrooms, and tuna mixture and serve it on a bed of lettuce or on whole-wheat bread.

Nutritional Information Per Serving

Calories 285 | Carbohydrate 32 g. | Fat 6 g. | Protein 27 g. | Fiber 6 g.

Nutritional Information Per Serving of Tuna Salad

Calories 155 | Carbohydrate 6 g. | Fat 5 g. | Protein 21 g. | Fiber 1 g.

Mediterranean Turkey Sandwich

The varied textures and flavors from the sun-dried tomatoes, avocado, and red peppers add interest to this sandwich.

3 tablespoons nonfat mayonnaise

1 tablespoon sun-dried tomato paste

8 thin slices multigrain bread

6 ounces oven-roasted or smoked sliced
  deli turkey breast, about 8 slices

½ avocado, peeled and pitted

½ large cucumber, unpeeled

½ cup roasted red bell pepper strips

1 cup baby spinach

1. Stir the mayonnaise and tomato paste together.

2. Spread 1 tablespoon of the mayonnaise mixture on each of 4 slices of the bread. Divide the turkey among the bread slices.

3. Cut the avocado and cucumber into 8 slices each. Top the turkey with 2 slices of avocado and cucumber.

4. Divide the pepper strips among the 4 sandwiches. Top each with ¼ cup spinach and a slice of multigrain bread.

YIELD: 4 servings

Nutritional Information Per Serving

Calories 300 | Carbohydrate 41 g. | Fat 7 g. | Protein 19 g. | Fiber 7 g.

Open-Faced Roast Beef Sandwich

Using only one slice of rye bread and adding lots of peppers and onions—lowered the calorie density of this sandwich.

*1½ cups sliced bell peppers, any
   combination of red, yellow, and/or green*
1 cup sliced mushrooms, about 2½ ounces
¾ cup sliced red onions
2 tablespoons reduced-fat mayonnaise
*2 teaspoons prepared horseradish, drained,
   or to taste*

4 thin slices rye bread
*8 ounces thinly sliced, lean, deli roast beef,
   about 10 slices*
4 tablespoons shredded Swiss cheese

1. Preheat the broiler.

2. In a nonstick skillet coated with cooking spray, sauté the peppers, mushrooms, and onions over medium heat for 5 minutes, or until slightly tender.

3. Combine the mayonnaise and horseradish and spread evenly over the rye slices.

4. Divide the roast beef among the slices of bread.

5. Divide the sautéed vegetables evenly over the sandwiches and top each with 1 tablespoon cheese.

6. Place the sandwiches on a baking sheet and broil until the cheese melts.

YIELD: 4 servings.

COOK'S NOTE: Chicken or turkey breast can be substituted for the roast beef; omit the horseradish.

Nutritional Information Per Serving

Calories 200 | Carbohydrate 19 g. | Fat 8 g. | Protein 15 g. | Fiber 2 g.

7 Salads and Salad Dressings

Dr. Rolls' Top Volumetrics Tips

1. Keep the proportion of vegetables high, and the fat down by carefully selecting the type of dressing and reducing the amount of dressing, cheese and croutons.
2. Add lean protein such as grilled chicken breast, chickpeas, lentils, or white beans for added satiety, especially if the salad is your main course.
3. Experiment with fat-free flavorings such as mustard, fresh herbs, Worcestershire sauce, citrus zest or minced garlic.

Volumterics Salad, page 66

Charlie's Greek Salad

This is a rustic side salad based on one my friend, Charlie was served during a trip to Athens. The feta cheese, although not in the original, adds another layer of flavor.

½ teaspoon salt
Freshly ground black pepper
1 tablespoon fresh lemon juice
1 tablespoon extra-virgin olive oil
2 cups scrubbed, unpeeled, and unseeded cucumber, quartered lengthwise, and

cut crosswise into ½-inch pieces, about ½ pound
2 cups cored tomatoes cut into ½-inch cubes
¼ cup chopped fresh oregano
¼ cup crumbled, nonfat feta cheese

1. Whisk the salt, several grindings of pepper, lemon juice, and oil in a large bowl. Add the cucumber, tomatoes, oregano, and feta. Toss gently, but well.

YIELD: 4 servings of ¾ cup each

COOK'S NOTE: This dish is best when tomatoes and cucumbers are at their peak.

Nutritional Information Per Serving

Calories 80 | Carbohydrate 6 g. | Fat 6 g. | Protein 2 g. | Fiber 1 g.

For an 80-calorie salad

TRADITIONAL	How we lowered calorie density	VOLUMETRICS
Greek salad	▸ Reduced oil ▸ Substituted nonfat feta cheese ▸ Omitted cured olives ▸ Increased the veggies	Charlie's Greek Salad

Volumetrics Salad

This is the salad used in one of the research studies at my lab. Serve this salad as a first course and it will fill you up so that you eat less during the rest of the meal.

8 cups mixed salad greens

1 cup peeled, shredded carrots

1 cup diced celery

1 cup cored, diced tomatoes

1 cup scrubbed, unpeeled diced cucumber

6 tablespoons shredded nonfat mozzarella cheese

¾ cup Italian Dressing (page 67)

1. Mix all the vegetables in a large bowl.

2. Add the mozzarella and Italian Dressing and toss well.

3. Divide the mixture among 4 salad bowls or plates.

YIELD: 4 servings of 3 cups each

COOK'S NOTE: This recipe uses the low-fat Italian Dressing (page 67) rather than a nonfat Italian dressing. If you prefer a nonfat dressing, try one of the commercially available nonfat Italian dressings.

Nutritional Information Per Serving

Calories 100 | Carbohydrate 16 g. | Fat 2 g. | Protein 5 g. | Fiber 4 g.

For a 100-calorie salad

TRADITIONAL	How we lowered calorie density	VOLUMETRICS
Tossed salad	‣ Used low-fat Italian dressing and reduced-fat cheese ‣ Added more vegetables	Volumetrics Salad

Italian Dressing

3 tablespoons white-wine vinegar
1 tablespoon extra-virgin olive oil

¼ teaspoon salt
Pinch freshly ground black pepper

1. Place all the ingredients and 2 tablespoons water in a screw-top jar. Shake vigorously until blended.

YIELD: 4 servings of 1½ tablespoons each

Nutritional Information Per Serving

Calories 45 | Carbohydrate 3 g. | Fat 4 g. | Protein 0 g. | Fiber 0 g.

Tuna and White Bean Salad

Serve this light, flavorful, and slightly tart salad with soup for lunch.

3 tablespoons lemon juice
1 tablespoon extra-virgin olive oil
1 teaspoon minced garlic
1 teaspoon Dijon mustard
½ teaspoon salt
Freshly ground black pepper
1 cup canned cannellini beans,
  rinsed and drained

½ cup chopped red onions
¼ cup pitted, chopped Niçoise olives
2 cups peeled, seeded, and diced tomatoes
3 cups baby spinach
1 12-ounce can solid white tuna,
  packed in water, drained and flaked

1. Whisk the lemon juice, oil, garlic, mustard, salt, several grindings of black pepper, and 2 tablespoons water in a large bowl.

2. Place the rest of the ingredients in the bowl and toss to coat with dressing.

YIELD: 4 servings of 1¾ cups each

COOK'S NOTE: Any white bean can be substituted for the cannellini. Other cured olives such as kalamata can be used in place of the Niçoise.

Nutritional Information Per Serving

Calories 200 | Carbohydrate 16 g. | Fat 7 g. | Protein 24 g. | Fiber 6 g.

For a 200-calorie salad

TRADITIONAL	How we lowered calorie density	VOLUMETRICS
Salad Niçoise	▸ Decreased oil ▸ Used tuna packed in water ▸ Added more vegetables	Tuna and White Bean Salad

Insalata Mista

Radicchio adds a vivid red accent and a peppery flavor to this side salad.

1 fennel bulb, about 1¼ pounds
4 cups torn Boston lettuce
3 cups torn radicchio
1 tablespoon extra-virgin olive oil

¼ teaspoon salt
Pinch freshly ground black pepper
3 to 4 tablespoons freshly squeezed
  lemon juice

1. Remove the fennel stalks and finely chop enough of the fronds to measure 2 tablespoons. Cut the bulbs in quarters lengthwise. Cut out and discard the core. Cut each quarter crosswise into thin slices.

2. In a large bowl, toss the fennel, fennel fronds, Boston lettuce, and radicchio with the oil, salt, and pepper. Add 3 tablespoons lemon juice and toss again. Taste and add more lemon juice, if desired.

3. Divide the salad among 4 salad plates or bowls.

YIELD: 4 servings of 1¾ cups each

Nutritional Information Per Serving

Calories 60 | Carbohydrate 7g. | Fat 4 g. | Protein 1 g. | Fiber 3 g.

Fennel, Orange, and Arugula Salad

Oranges, along with the distinctive taste of arugula and the crunchy texture of the fennel, make this a bright and refreshing side salad.

2 large navel oranges

1 tablespoon orange juice

1 tablespoon extra-virgin olive oil

¼ teaspoon salt

Pinch freshly ground black pepper

1 fennel bulb, about 1¼ pounds

4 cups shredded arugula

1. Grate 2 teaspoons orange zest. Peel the oranges, making sure to remove all the bitter white pith. Cut the flesh into ½" thick slices and cut the slices crosswise into cubes.

2. Whisk the zest, orange juice, oil, salt, and pepper in a large bowl.

3. Remove the fennel stalks and chop enough of the fronds to measure 1 tablespoon. Cut the bulb lengthwise into quarters. Cut out and discard the core. Cut each quarter crosswise into thin slices.

4. Toss the orange cubes, fennel, fennel fronds, and arugula with the dressing.

YIELD: 4 servings of 1 cup each

Nutritional Information Per Serving

Calories 80 | Carbohydrate 13 g. | Fat 4 g. | Protein 2 g. | Fiber 4 g.

8 Sides

Dr. Rolls' Top Volumetrics Tips

1. Add herbs and lemon juice to complement and add flavor to vegetable side dishes without adding extra fat.
2. Try roasted vegetables. Roasting slightly caramelizes vegetables and brings out their full flavor.
3. Stir-fry vegetables for a quick side dish with fresh crisp textures and flavors using only a little fat.

Garlic-Roasted Vegetables, page 76

Minted Broccoli

The mint and lemon juice complement the taste of broccoli, so it can be enjoyed without added fat. The calorie density is so low you can eat as much as you like.

1 pound broccoli
¾ teaspoon salt
2 tablespoons lemon juice

Freshly ground black pepper
1 tablespoon chopped fresh mint

1. Remove the tough ends of the broccoli stems, peel the stems, and cut the broccoli into ½-inch-thick spears.

2. Bring 1 inch of water to a boil in a large saucepan. Add ½ teaspoon salt and the broccoli and simmer, covered, for 5 minutes. Drain the broccoli and return it to the pan.

3. Place the pan over very low heat. Sprinkle with the lemon juice, ¼ teaspoon of salt, a few grindings of black pepper, and the mint. Toss gently to combine.

YIELD: 4 servings of ¾ cup each

COOK'S NOTE: Try using your favorite fresh herb or combination of herbs in place of the mint.

Nutritional Information Per Serving

Calories 35 | Carbohydrate 7 g. | Fat 1 g. | Protein 3 g. | Fiber 1 g.

For a 35-calorie side dish

TRADITIONAL	How we lowered calorie density	VOLUMETRICS
Broccoli with cheese sauce	▸ Omitted cheese sauce ▸ Used fresh herbs for flavor	Minted Broccoli

Garlic-Roasted Vegetables

Roasting slightly caramelizes the vegetables and brings out their full flavor in this side dish.

1 cup cauliflowerettes

1 cup broccoli florets

2 cups 1-inch-thick slices of zucchini

1½ cups 1-inch-long carrot sticks

1½ cups thickly sliced onions

1½ cups unpeeled boiling potatoes, cut into
   1-inch cubes

1 teaspoon chopped garlic

1 teaspoon dried thyme

½ teaspoon salt

¼ teaspoon freshly ground black pepper

¼ cup chopped fresh flat-leaf parsley

1. Preheat the oven to 400 degrees.

2. Lightly coat a 9-by-13-inch baking dish with cooking spray.

3. Place all the ingredients, except the parsley, in the baking dish and toss well. Arrange in an even layer and lightly coat with cooking spray. Bake for 40 to 45 minutes, or until potatoes are tender.

4. Serve sprinkled with the parsley.

YIELD: 4 servings of 1¾ cups each

COOK'S NOTE: Other vegetables, such as bell peppers, yellow squash, or eggplant can be substituted for the cauliflower and broccoli. Experiment with your favorites.

Nutritional Information Per Serving

Calories 90 | Carbohydrate 19 g. | Fat 1 g. | Protein 3 g. | Fiber 4 g.

For a 90-calorie side dish

TRADITIONAL	How we lowered calorie density	VOLUMETRICS
Breaded deep-fried vegetables	▶ Omitted the breading ▶ Oven-roasted instead of deep fried ▶ Used garlic for flavor	Garlic-Roasted Vegetables

Stir-Fried Green Beans

Stir-frying is a way to quickly prepare dishes with fresh, crisp textures and flavors using only a little fat.

1½ teaspoons sesame oil

1½ pounds green beans, trimmed and cut
  into 1-inch pieces

1½ teaspoons reduced-sodium soy sauce

1 teaspoon sugar

1. Heat the oil over medium-high heat in a large nonstick skillet or wok. Add the green beans and stir-fry 3 minutes. Add the soy sauce and stir-fry 1 minute. Add the sugar and stir-fry 30 seconds.

YIELD: 4 servings of 1¼ cups each

COOK'S NOTE: Thin asparagus can be substituted for the green beans. Sliced bamboo shoots provide an attractive garnish.

Nutritional Information Per Serving

Calories 65 | Carbohydrate 12 g. | Fat 2 g. | Protein 3 g. | Fiber 5 g.

For a 65-calorie side dish

TRADITIONAL	How we lowered calorie density	VOLUMETRICS
Green-bean casserole	▸ Omitted cream soup ▸ Omitted fried onions ▸ Used a small amount of sesame oil to increase flavor	Stir-Fried Green Beans

9 Meatless

Dr. Rolls' Top Volumetrics Tips

1. Increase the amount of vegetables and decrease the amount of fat added to your favorite pasta dishes.
2. Choose whole grain or wheat blended pastas to boost your fiber intake and increase satiety.
3. Sneak beans or split peas into stews and other mixed dishes.

Charlie's Pasta Primavera, page 84

Bulgur and Vegetable Stuffed Peppers

Bulgur provides the extra fiber associated with whole grains, and gives this dish a hearty texture. Enjoy this as a side dish, or double the portion to make a main dish.

1 cup vegetable broth
⅔ cup bulgur
4 red, yellow, or orange bell peppers, about
   2 pounds
½ cup finely chopped celery
¼ cup chopped scallions
½ cup diced mushrooms, about 2 ounces

½ cup peeled, shredded carrots
¼ cup grated Parmesan cheese
½ teaspoon dried thyme
½ teaspoon dried oregano
½ teaspoon salt
Pinch cayenne

For a 150-calorie side dish

TRADITIONAL	How we lowered calorie density	VOLUMETRICS
Sausage-stuffed peppers	▸ Decreased amount of oil ▸ Omitted sausage ▸ Added bulgur and vegetables	Bulgur and Vegetable Stuffed Peppers

1. Bring the broth and bulgur to a boil in a 2-quart saucepan, stirring constantly. Reduce the heat and simmer, covered, 10 minutes. Fluff with a fork and put in a large bowl.

2. Preheat the oven to 375 degrees.

3. Lightly coat an 8-by-8-inch baking dish with cooking spray.

4. Cut the tops off the bell peppers and remove the core and seeds. Cut a very thin slice off the bottom of the bell peppers so they will stand upright.

5. Cook the peppers, in a large pot of boiling water, 3 minutes. Remove the peppers and drain, inverted, on paper towels.

6. Combine the remaining ingredients with the bulgur. Divide the mixture among the peppers. Place the peppers upright in the baking dish and bake 15 to 20 minutes.

YIELD: 4 servings

COOK'S NOTE: Bulgur is available in the natural-food section of some supermarkets and in specialty grocery stores.

Nutritional Information Per Serving

Calories 150 | Carbohydrate 27 g. | Fat 3 g. | Protein 8 g. | Fiber 8 g.

Charlie's Pasta Primavera

There are lots of combinations of vegetables that work with pasta. Charlie has tried many, but this is his favorite. It is delicious without the usual butter or cream.

1 tablespoon extra-virgin olive oil
1 cup seeded, chopped bell peppers of
   any color
1 cup chopped onions
1 teaspoon chopped garlic
2 cups diced zucchini
1 pound thin asparagus, trimmed and
   cut into 1-inch lengths

2 cups cored, chopped fresh tomatoes
2 tablespoons fresh oregano
1 teaspoon salt
Pinch freshly ground black pepper
8 ounces dry whole-wheat penne
4 cups baby spinach
4 tablespoons grated Parmesan cheese

For a 345-calorie entrée

TRADITIONAL	How we lowered calorie density	VOLUMETRICS
Pasta primavera	▸ Decreased the amount of pasta ▸ Increased the amount of veggies ▸ Omitted cream sauce	Charlie's Pasta Primavera

1. Heat the oil in a large nonstick skillet over medium heat. Add the bell peppers, onions, and garlic and cook, stirring frequently, 5 minutes.

2. Add the zucchini, asparagus, tomatoes, oregano, salt, and pepper. Stir well. Reduce the heat to medium-low and cook, uncovered, 10 to 15 minutes, stirring occasionally. Keep the sauce warm over low heat.

3. Cook the penne as directed on the package. Reserve ½ cup cooking water and drain the pasta.

4. Add the penne and spinach to the sauce and stir thoroughly. Let the mixture sit over low heat about 1 minute.

5. Stir in about ¼ cup reserved cooking water. Add more if the mixture looks dry.

6. Divide the pasta among 4 dinner plates or shallow bowls and sprinkle with Parmesan.

YIELD: 4 servings of 3 cups each

COOK'S NOTE: Any medium whole-wheat pasta can be substituted for the penne, such as zitti, rotelle, or farfalle. Fresh green beans cut into 1-inch lengths can be substituted for the asparagus.

Nutritional Information Per Serving

Calories 345 | Carbohydrate 59 g. | Fat 7 g. | Protein 15 g. | Fiber 10 g.

Veggie-Stuffed Macaroni and Cheese

This volumetric main course shows that you can enjoy the ultimate comfort food while managing your weight.

8 ounces dry, whole-wheat elbow macaroni, fusilli, or penne
2 tablespoons whole-wheat breadcrumbs
1 teaspoon melted butter
¼ teaspoon paprika
1¾ cups nonfat milk
3 tablespoons all-purpose flour
2 cups shredded, reduced-fat Cheddar cheese
1 cup 1 percent fat cottage cheese

¼ cup grated Parmesan cheese
Pinch grated nutmeg
½ teaspoon salt
Pinch freshly ground black pepper
6 cups shredded fresh spinach, about 1 pound
1½ cups canned diced tomatoes, with liquid

1. Preheat the oven to 375 degrees.

2. Lightly coat a 9-by-13-inch baking dish with cooking spray.

3. Cook the pasta according to the package directions. Drain and set aside.

4. Mix the breadcrumbs, butter, and paprika in a small bowl and set aside.

5. Heat 1½ cups milk in a 4- to 5-quart nonstick saucepan over medium-high heat until steaming.

6. Whisk the remaining ¼ cup milk and the flour in a small bowl until smooth. Add to the hot milk and cook, whisking constantly, until the sauce thickens and simmers, 3 to 7 minutes. Remove the pan from the heat.

7. Add the Cheddar to the white sauce and stir until the cheese is melted. Stir in the cottage cheese, Parmesan, nutmeg, salt, and pepper. Stir the pasta into the cheese sauce.

8. Spread half of the pasta mixture into the baking dish. Place the spinach evenly on

top, then the diced tomatoes. Spread the remaining pasta mixture over the tomatoes and sprinkle with the breadcrumb mixture.

9. Bake until bubbly and golden, 25 to 30 minutes.

YIELD: 6 servings of 1½ cups each

COOK'S NOTE: Two cups chopped fresh broccoli florets can be substituted for the spinach. Make breadcrumbs by pulverizing torn pieces of bread in a food processor or blender.

Nutritional Information Per Serving

Calories 330 | Carbohydrate 38 g. | Fat 9 g. | Protein 25 g. | Fiber 5 g.

For a 330-calorie entrée

TRADITIONAL	How we lowered calorie density	VOLUMETRICS
Macaroni and cheese	▸ Used whole-wheat pasta, nonfat milk, and reduced-fat cheese ▸ Reduced the amount of butter and cheese ▸ Added vegetables	Veggie-Stuffed Macaroni and Cheese

Garden-Fresh Vegetable Pizza

This recipe makes an eye-catching pizza. The vegetables complement the traditional tomatoes and mozzarella.

1 tablespoon extra-virgin olive oil
1 cup thinly sliced leeks, white part only
1 teaspoon minced garlic
1 cup peeled, grated carrots
9 ounces packaged wheat pizza dough
2 medium tomatoes, cored and cut into
    1/4-inch slices
1/2 cup thinly sliced zucchini

1 cup thin asparagus, cut into 1-inch-long
    pieces
Salt
Freshly ground black pepper
1/2 cup shredded, nonfat mozzarella cheese

1. Preheat the oven to 375 degrees.

2. Heat the oil in a nonstick skillet over medium heat. Add the leeks and garlic and cook, stirring occasionally, 4 minutes. Stir in the carrots and cook 1 minute. Remove the skillet from the heat and set aside.

3. Stretch the dough out in a 12-inch pizza pan or roll out into a 12-inch round on a baking sheet.

4. Spread the leek mixture onto the dough, leaving a 1/2-inch border.

5. Arrange the tomato slices around the outside edge of the leek mixture and lay the zucchini slices in the center. Place the asparagus on top of the tomatoes. Season lightly with the salt and pepper. Sprinkle the mozzarella over the pizza.

6. Bake until the crust is golden, about 15 to 20 minutes. Cut the pizza into 4 wedges.

YIELD: 4 servings.

COOK'S NOTE: Packaged wheat pizza dough made with whole-wheat flour is available in larger supermarkets. If packaged pizza dough is not available at your local store, a pre-made crust can be used, but it will increase the calorie level by approximately 100 calories per serving.

Nutritional Information Per Serving

Calories 285 | Carbohydrate 41 g. | Fat 9 g. | Protein 13 g. | Fiber 5 g.

10 Beef

Dr. Rolls' Top Volumetrics Tips

1. Keep meat portions to around 2-3 ounces per serving.
2. Trim fat from meat and choose cuts with the least marbling.
3. Choose the leanest ground beef and and remove fat drippings.

Old World Goulash, page 92

Old World Goulash

This volumetric version of the traditional Hungarian beef stew provides satisfying portions with lots of vegetables.

1 tablespoon extra-virgin olive oil

1 pound well-trimmed, boneless beef round roast, cut into 1-inch pieces

½ teaspoon salt

¼ teaspoon freshly ground black pepper

1 cup chopped onions

1 teaspoon chopped garlic

2 cups sliced mushrooms, about ⅓ pound

1 cup nonfat, reduced-sodium beef broth

2 cups peeled, diced boiling potatoes, about 1 pound

2 cups peeled, thinly sliced carrots

1 cup sliced celery

12 ounces trimmed green beans, cut into 1-inch lengths

2 tablespoons paprika

½ teaspoon dried thyme

1 tablespoon tomato paste

2 tablespoons cornstarch

2 tablespoons dry red wine

1. Lightly coat a 4- to 5-quart heavy pot or Dutch oven with cooking spray. Add the oil and heat over medium-high heat. Add the beef, salt, and pepper. Cook, stirring occasionally, until the beef browns, 6 to 8 minutes.

2. Add the onions, garlic, and mushrooms and cook 5 minutes.

3. Add the broth, and enough water to barely cover the ingredients in the pot. Bring to a simmer, stirring occasionally. Cover the pot and cook 45 minutes, stirring occasionally.

4. Add the potatoes, carrots, celery, beans, paprika, thyme, and tomato paste and stir well. Add more water, if necessary, to barely cover. Simmer, uncovered, 45 minutes, stirring occasionally. Add additional water, if necessary, to prevent the stew from drying out.

5. Whisk the cornstarch and wine in a small bowl until smooth. Stir the mixture into the goulash and cook over medium-high heat, stirring occasionally, until slightly thickened and bubbly, about 3 minutes. Taste the sauce and season with salt and pepper, if necessary.

YIELD: 4 servings of 2½ cups each

COOK'S NOTE: The paprika provides the distinctive flavor and color of this dish so be sure it is fresh. The goulash is delicious by itself, but it is often served with noodles. Try whole-wheat, broad egg noodles, or short pasta such as whole-wheat fusilli or penne.

Nutritional Information Per Serving
Calories 335 | Carbohydrate 32 g. | Fat 11 g. | Protein 30 g. | Fiber 10 g.

For a 335-calorie entrée

TRADITIONAL	How we lowered calorie density	VOLUMETRICS
Traditional beef goulash	▶ Used less oil to sauté ▶ Omitted sour cream ▶ Used lean beef and twice as many vegetables	Old World Goulash

Garden Chili

This volumetric version of traditional chili has visual appeal and a lower calorie density.

1 pound 95 percent lean ground beef
2 cups chopped onions
3 tablespoons chopped garlic
1 cup seeded, chopped green bell peppers
¾ teaspoon salt
¼ teaspoon freshly ground black pepper
3 tablespoons chili powder
2 teaspoons cumin

3 cups canned crushed tomatoes
3 cups nonfat, reduced-sodium beef broth
3 cups canned dark-red kidney beans, rinsed and drained
1 cup chopped celery
2 cups peeled, shredded carrots
1 cup chopped zucchini
1 tablespoon hot-pepper sauce

1. Lightly coat a 4- to 5-quart pot with cooking spray. Heat the pot over medium-high heat until hot. Crumble the beef into the pot and add the onions, garlic, bell peppers, salt, and pepper. Cook, stirring occasionally, until the beef loses its raw color. Drain the liquid from the pot.

2. Reduce the heat to medium and stir in the chili powder and cumin. Add the remaining ingredients and 1 cup water, and bring to a boil, stirring. Cover the pot, reduce the heat, and simmer 45 minutes, stirring occasionally.

YIELD: 8 servings of 1¾ cups each

COOK'S NOTE: Leftover chili is great as a topping for a baked potato.

Nutritional Information Per Serving

Calories 315 | Carbohydrate 31 g. | Fat 11 g. | Protein 25 g. | Fiber 11 g.

For a 315-calorie entrée

TRADITIONAL	How we lowered calorie density	VOLUMETRICS
Beef chili	▸ Used lean ground beef and no oil ▸ Added more veggies	Garden Chili

Santa Fe Steak Salad with Lime-Cilantro Dressing

You can eat steak when following Volumetrics, just watch your portion, and combine it with lots of veggies to reduce the calorie density. Serve this main dish salad for lunch or dinner.

½ cup lime juice

3 tablespoons extra-virgin olive oil

½ cup chopped fresh cilantro

1 tablespoon chopped garlic

2 teaspoons sugar

1 teaspoon cumin

⅛ teaspoon cayenne

1 pound flank steak, cut diagonally against the grain into ¼-inch thick pieces

8 cups mixed salad greens

1 cup peeled, diced jicama

1 seeded red or green bell pepper, sliced

½ cup chopped red onions

¼ cup chopped green olives

1 cup halved cherry tomatoes

½ cup canned dark-red kidney beans, rinsed and drained

½ cup canned corn, drained

¾ cup diced avocado

½ cup shredded, reduced-fat Mexican-blend cheese

1 cup prepared tomato salsa

1. Combine the lime juice, oil, cilantro, garlic, sugar, cumin, cayenne, and ½ cup of water in a blender. Blend on high until smooth. Set the Lime-Cilantro Dressing aside.

2. Marinate the steak in the dressing for 1 hour.

3. Place a large skillet coated with cooking spray over medium-high heat. When it is hot, add the meat and marinade, and cook, stirring, 3 to 4 minutes, or until the meat is no longer pink. Transfer the meat to a plate and cover.

4. Divide the greens among 4 plates.

5. Mix the jicama, bell peppers, onions, olives, tomatoes, beans, corn, and avocado in a bowl.

6. Divide the jicama mixture among the plates and top with the cheese, salsa, and steak.

YIELD: 4 servings of 3½ cups each

COOK'S NOTE: Jicama, also known as *Mexican potato,* can be found in the produce section of large supermarkets and specialty grocery stores. It is a crunchy tuber that adds wonderful flavor and texture to salads. (When used as a dressing for salad, Lime-Cilantro Dressing yields 12 servings of 1½ tablespoons each.)

Nutritional Information Per Serving

Calories 400 | Carbohydrate 29 g. | Fat 18 g. | Protein 33 g. | Fiber 10 g.

Nutritional Information Per 1½ Tablespoon Serving of Dressing

Calories 40 | Carbohydrate 2 g. | Fat 4 g. | Protein 0 g. | Fiber 0 g.

11 Fish and Shellfish

Dr. Rolls' Top Volumetrics Tips

1. Add more fish to your diet, calorie for calorie, fish has been shown to enhance satiety more than chicken or beef.
2. Select omega-3 fatty acid rich fish twice a week and pair it with lots of vegetables. Grill the fish or mix it into dishes that don't require much additional fat.
3. Instead of breading and frying fish and shellfish, be sure to use cooking methods with little added fat.

Shrimp Fried Rice, page 102

Baked Tilapia with Sautéed Vegetables

Try this simple method of cooking fish fillets for a colorful and delicious main dish.

1 to 1½ pounds tilapia fillets
½ cup orange juice
2 teaspoons vegetable oil
¼ teaspoon salt
1 cup chopped green bell peppers

¾ cup halved and sliced onions
2 teaspoons minced garlic
1½ cups canned diced tomatoes, with
  liquid

For a 160-calorie entrée

TRADITIONAL	How we lowered calorie density	VOLUMETRICS
Breaded and fried fish	▸ Omitted the breading ▸ Baked the fish instead of frying ▸ Added vegetables	Baked Tilapia with Sautéed Vegetables

1. Preheat the oven to 350 degrees. Lightly coat a baking dish large enough to accommodate the fillets in one layer with cooking spray.

2. Rinse the fillets under cold water, pat dry, and place them in the baking dish in a single layer, skin side down.

3. Combine 2 tablespoons orange juice with 1 teaspoon oil and sprinkle over the fillets. Sprinkle with salt and bake 15 to 20 minutes, or until the fish is flaky and no longer translucent.

4. Lightly coat a large skillet with cooking spray, add remaining 1 teaspoon oil and heat over medium-high heat. Add the bell peppers and onions and cook, stirring occasionally, 5 minutes. Add the remaining orange juice, garlic, and tomatoes. Cook, stirring occasionally, 2 minutes, or until heated through.

5. Divide the fillets among 4 plates and spoon the sauce over them.

YIELD: 4 servings

COOK'S NOTE: Other fish choices are flounder, cod, red snapper, or sole. Lemon juice or dry white wine can be substituted for the orange juice.

Nutritional Information Per Serving

Calories 160 | Carbohydrate 10 g. | Fat 3 g. | Protein 22 g. | Fiber 2 g.

Shrimp Fried Rice

The rich taste of the dark sesame oil adds a distinctive flavor to this quick stir-fry meal.

3 teaspoons dark sesame oil
¾ pound small shrimp, shelled and
   deveined
2 teaspoons chopped garlic
2 teaspoons chopped fresh ginger
1 cup peeled, finely chopped carrots
1 cup small broccoli florets
¼ cup chopped scallions
1 cup seeded, chopped red or green bell
   peppers

1 cup frozen peas, thawed
2 cups cooked brown rice
1 tablespoon reduced-sodium soy sauce
1 tablespoon hoisin sauce
Pinch cayenne
1 egg
1 egg white

1. Heat 1 teaspoon oil in a large nonstick skillet or wok over medium-high heat. Add the shrimp, garlic, and ginger and stir-fry 3 minutes, or until the shrimp are pink and opaque. Transfer the shrimp to a plate and cover to keep warm.

2. Add 2 teaspoons oil to the skillet and stir-fry the carrots, broccoli, scallions, bell peppers, and peas 2 minutes.

3. Add the rice, soy sauce, hoisin sauce, cayenne, and shrimp and stir-fry 3 minutes, or until heated through.

4. Combine the egg and egg white in a small bowl. Add the eggs to the skillet and cook, stirring occasionally, until the eggs are set.

YIELD: 4 servings of 1½ cups each

COOK'S NOTE: Substitute 6 ounces of tofu for the shrimp for a vegetarian version.

Nutritional Information Per Serving

Calories 325 | Carbohydrate 39 g. | Fat 8 g. | Protein 26 g. | Fiber 6 g.

For a 325-calorie entrée

TRADITIONAL	How we lowered calorie density	VOLUMETRICS
Stir-fried shrimp with peanuts	▸ Decreased oil ▸ Omitted nuts ▸ Added more vegetables	Shrimp Fried Rice

Fillet of Sole and Vegetable Parcels

Open these parcels at the table to allow the diner to enjoy the heady aroma of the contents.

2 medium zucchini, about ¾ pound
1 trimmed well-washed medium leek
½ pound trimmed thin asparagus
4 sole fillets, about 5 ounces each
4 tablespoons dry white wine

8 thin slices lemon
¼ cup chopped fresh dill
2 teaspoons chopped garlic
Salt
Freshly ground black pepper

1. Preheat the oven to 400 degrees.

2. Remove the ends of each zucchini. Using a broad vegetable peeler or mandolin, remove long, thin slices of the zucchini and set aside.

3. Cut the white part of the leek into julienne strips and the asparagus into 2-inch long pieces and set aside. Cut out 4 13-by-13-inch pieces of parchment paper.

4. Place 1 fillet on each of the parchment pieces. Sprinkle with the wine and top each with 2 lemon slices. Divide the zucchini, leeks, and asparagus over the fillets and sprinkle with the dill and garlic. Season lightly with salt and pepper.

5. Bring up the top and bottom sides of each piece of parchment paper and fold the edges over to form a tight seam. Twist the ends and tuck under the parcel.

6. Place the parcels on a baking sheet and bake 20 minutes. Serve the parcels unopened.

YIELD: 4 servings

COOK'S NOTE: Flounder or tilapia fillet can be substituted for the sole. Vegetable broth can be used in place of wine.

Nutritional Information Per Serving

Calories 230 | Carbohydrate 9 g. | Fat 8 g. | Protein 30 g. | Fiber 3 g.

Poach-Roast Salmon with Yogurt and Dill Sauce

This is a simple and almost foolproof method of cooking salmon fillets so that they remain moist.

½ cup nonfat plain yogurt
½ teaspoon minced garlic
1 tablespoon minced onions
1 tablespoon drained capers, chopped if
   large
3 tablespoons lemon juice

1 tablespoon chopped fresh dill
1 pound salmon fillet, cut crosswise into
   4 equal portions
¼ teaspoon salt
Pinch freshly ground black pepper
4 lemon wedges

1. Preheat the oven to 400 degrees.

2. In a small bowl, stir the yogurt, garlic, onions, capers, 1 tablespoon lemon juice, and ½ tablespoon dill until smooth. Set the Yogurt and Dill Sauce aside.

3. Lightly coat an 8- by 12-inch glass baking dish with cooking spray.

4. Place the salmon, skin-side down, in the dish. Sprinkle with 2 tablespoons lemon juice. Season with salt, pepper, and ½ tablespoon dill. Cover the dish tightly with foil and bake 15 to 25 minutes until fish is flaky and no longer translucent.

5. Divide the salmon among 4 dinner plates and garnish with 2 tablespoons of the sauce and a lemon wedge.

YIELD: 4 servings

Nutritional Information Per Serving

Calories 225 | Carbohydrate 4 g. | Fat 13 g. | Protein 24 g. | Fiber 0 g.

Nutritional Information Per Serving of Yogurt and Dill Sauce

Calories 15 | Carbohydrate 2 g. | Fat 1 g. | Protein 1 g. | Fiber 1 g.

 12 Poultry

Dr. Rolls' Top Volumetrics Tips

1. Cook poultry with the skin on to help the meat stay juicy (very little of the fat from the skin is absorbed while cooking). Just remove the skin before eating.
2. Check the label and choose ground poultry with the lowest fat content (some ground poultry can contain skin, again adding unnecessary fat and calories), or pick a lean piece of meat and ask to have it ground.
3. Select white meat because dark meat, even without the skin, contains more fat and calories.

Chicken Merlot, page 108

Chicken Merlot

This entrée evokes some of the traditional flavors of French country cooking.

4 skinless, boneless chicken breast halves,
    4 to 6 ounces each
¼ cup all-purpose flour
1 teaspoon dried thyme
½ teaspoon salt
2 teaspoons extra-virgin olive oil
3 cups quartered mushrooms, about ½
    pound

2 cups peeled, sliced carrots
4 pieces Canadian bacon, cut into ¼-inch
    wide slices
⅔ cup Merlot or other dry red wine
⅔ cup nonfat, reduced-sodium chicken
    broth
2 teaspoons tomato paste
¼ cup chopped fresh flat-leaf parsley

For a 240-calorie entrée

TRADITIONAL	How we lowered calorie density	VOLUMETRICS
Coq au vin	▸ Used skinless, white chicken instead of dark meat ▸ Used less oil ▸ Added more veggies ▸ Used Canadian bacon instead of regular bacon	Chicken Merlot

1. Cut each chicken breast crosswise into 3 pieces.

2. Combine the flour, thyme, and salt in a resealable plastic bag and add the chicken pieces. Seal the bag and shake to coat chicken. Remove the chicken and shake off excess flour.

3. Lightly coat a large nonstick skillet with cooking spray. Add 1 teaspoon oil and heat over medium-high heat. Add the chicken and cook, stirring, about 5 minutes, or until the chicken is lightly browned on both sides. Remove the chicken and set it aside.

4. Add 1 teaspoon oil to the skillet and sauté the mushrooms, carrots, and bacon 2 minutes. Stir in the wine, broth, and tomato paste, and cook, stirring occasionally, 10 minutes.

5. Return the chicken to the skillet and cook 4 to 5 minutes, or until it is no longer pink in the center.

6. Divide the chicken mixture among 4 plates, sprinkle with the parsley, and serve.

YIELD: 4 servings

COOK'S NOTE: Try serving the chicken with boiled potatoes, whole-wheat noodles, or short whole-wheat pasta, such as fusilli or penne.

Nutritional Information Per Serving

Calories 240 | Carbohydrate 15 g. | Fat 6 g. | Protein 26 g. | Fiber 3 g.

South of the Border Chicken Stew

This zesty dish is a whole meal in one pot.

4 skinless, boneless chicken breast halves,
   4 to 6 ounces each
Salt
Freshly ground black pepper
2 tablespoons extra-virgin olive oil
1½ cups chopped onions
1 cup seeded, chopped green bell peppers
1 cup diced celery
1 teaspoon chopped garlic
2 teaspoons dried oregano

4 cups nonfat, reduced-sodium
   chicken broth
1½ cups frozen corn, thawed
1½ cups canned diced tomatoes, with
   liquid
3 cups baby spinach
¼ teaspoon hot-pepper sauce
½ cup nonfat plain yogurt
¼ cup chopped scallions

1. Cut the chicken into 1-inch chunks and season lightly with salt and pepper.

2. Heat 1 tablespoon of the oil in a 4- to 5-quart pot over medium-high heat. Lightly brown the chicken, stirring, about 5 minutes. Remove the chicken to a bowl.

3. Reduce the heat to medium and add 1 tablespoon oil, onions, bell peppers, celery, and garlic. Cook, stirring frequently, 5 minutes. Stir in the oregano, broth, and ½ teaspoon salt. Bring to a simmer and cook 10 minutes.

4. Stir in the corn, tomatoes, and chicken and simmer 10 minutes, stirring occasionally. Stir in the spinach and hot-pepper sauce.

5. Divide the stew among 4 bowls, and serve with the yogurt and scallions in small bowls on the side.

YIELD: 4 servings of 2½ cups each

Nutritional Information Per Serving

Calories 325 | Carbohydrate 24 g. | Fat 11 g. | Protein 34 g. | Fiber 6 g.

For a 325-calorie entrée

TRADITIONAL	How we lowered calorie density	VOLUMETRICS
Mexican stew	▸ Used skinless chicken breast instead of dark meat ▸ Decreased oil ▸ Added more vegetables ▸ Omitted tortilla chips	South of the Border Chicken Stew

Chicken Provençal

Cooking this entrée will fill your kitchen with the aromas of southern French cooking.

1 tablespoon extra-virgin olive oil
4 skinless, boneless chicken breast halves,
   4 to 6 ounces each
½ cup chopped onions
1 teaspoon chopped garlic
½ teaspoon salt
Pinch freshly ground black pepper

½ cup dry white wine
1½ cups canned diced tomatoes, with liquid
¼ cup chopped, pitted kalamata or other
   brine-cured olives
1 tablespoon chopped fresh oregano
1 tablespoon chopped fresh flat-leaf
   parsley

1. Heat the oil in a large nonstick skillet over medium heat. Add the chicken, onions, garlic, salt, and pepper. Sautée until the chicken is lightly browned, about 3 minutes on each side.

2. Add the wine and bring to a boil. Add the tomatoes, olives, and oregano and return to the boil. Reduce the heat to low, partially cover, and cook about 6 minutes, or until the chicken is no longer pink.

3. Transfer the chicken to a platter and keep warm. Cook the sauce 2 to 3 minutes, or until it has thickened slightly. Spoon the sauce over the chicken and sprinkle with parsley.

YIELD: 4 servings

COOK'S NOTE: Fresh marjoram is a good substitute for oregano.

Nutritional Information Per Serving

Calories 165 | Carbohydrate 7 g. | Fat 5 g. | Protein 18 g. | Fiber 1 g.

Stir-Fried Turkey with Crunchy Vegetables

This quick main dish uses turkey breast cutlets, a good source of lean protein.

2 teaspoons cornstarch
3 tablespoons soy sauce
1 teaspoon vegetable oil
3 slices fresh ginger, ⅛-inch thick
1 pound turkey breast cutlets, cut into
   ½-inch cubes
1 teaspoon sesame oil
1 cup shredded green cabbage

½ cup sliced onions
1 cup 1-inch-long celery sticks
1 cup 1-inch-long green bell pepper sticks
1 cup 1-inch-long carrot sticks
1 teaspoon chopped garlic
¼ teaspoon freshly ground black pepper
2 cups cooked brown rice

1. Mix the cornstarch with 4 tablespoons cold water in a small bowl to form a thin paste. Stir in the soy sauce and set aside.

2. Heat the vegetable oil in a large, nonstick skillet or wok over high heat. When the oil is hot, add the ginger and stir-fry 1 minute. Remove the ginger with a slotted spoon and discard.

3. Add the turkey to the skillet and stir-fry 3 minutes. Use a slotted spoon to transfer the turkey to a bowl, and set aside.

4. Reduce the heat to medium-high and add the sesame oil. Add the cabbage, onions, celery, bell pepper, carrot, garlic, and black pepper to the skillet and stir-fry 3 minutes.

5. Stir the sauce to recombine and add to the skillet along with the turkey and its juices and stir-fry 2 minutes.

6. Divide the rice and stir-fry mixture among 4 dinner plates.

YIELD: 4 servings of ½ cup rice and ¾ cup stir-fry each

Nutritional Information Per Serving

Calories 330 | Carbohydrate 34 g. | Fat 5 g. | Protein 31 g. | Fiber 5 g.

13 Desserts

Dr. Rolls' Top Volumetrics Tips

1. Dessert is an ideal time to add more fruit to your day. Most fruits are high in fiber and their high water content makes them very low in calorie density.
2. Add fresh, frozen, or canned fruits to dishes you already like (such as berries or bananas to yogurt).
3. Try grilling fruit. At your next barbecue, put tropical fruit such as pineapple and mango on skewers.

Fresh Fruit Parfait, page 120

Balsamic Berries

A few drops of aged balsamic vinegar bring out the flavor of the fruit—you won't taste the vinegar.

4 cups strawberries, about 1 pound
1 tablespoon sugar

¼ teaspoon aged balsamic vinegar

1. Wash, dry, hull, and quarter the strawberries lengthwise.

2. Put the strawberries into a large bowl. Add the sugar and balsamic vinegar and toss gently to combine. Refrigerate 1 hour.

3. Spoon the strawberries into chilled stemmed glasses or dessert bowls.

YIELD: 4 servings of 1 cup each

COOK'S NOTE: Aged Italian balsamic vinegar has a more intense flavor than many domestic varieties. Increase the amount to 1 teaspoon if you use the latter.

Nutritional Information Per Serving

Calories 55 | Carbohydrate 13 g. | Fat 0 g. | Protein 1 g. | Fiber 3 g.

For a 55-calorie dessert

TRADITIONAL	How we lowered calorie density	VOLUMETRICS
Strawberries and cream	▸ Substituted balsamic vinegar and a small amount of sugar for cream	Balsamic Berries

Ruby-Red Poached Pears with Raspberry Sauce

Create a light, but grand, finale by poaching one of autumn's most delicious fruits.

6 firm Bartlett pears with stems
1 quart cranberry-apple juice
1 tablespoon lemon juice
3 whole cloves
1 3-inch-long cinnamon stick
1½ cups unsweetened frozen raspberries,
* thawed*

2 tablespoons sugar
½ teaspoon orange liqueur or 1 tablespoon
* orange juice*
6 fresh mint sprigs

1. Carefully peel the pears, leaving the stems intact.

2. Place the juices, cloves, and cinnamon stick in a 4- to 5-quart pot. Lay the pears in the pot and bring to a simmer over medium heat. Simmer the pears, covered, 1 hour.

3. Remove the pot from the heat, uncover, and cool the pears in the liquid. Cover the pot and refrigerate the pears in the liquid overnight.

4. Puree the raspberries, sugar, and liqueur in a food processor or blender. Set the Raspberry Sauce aside.

5. Remove the pears from the liquid. Cut a thin slice from the bottom of each pear.

6. Spoon some of the raspberry sauce on a serving platter or 1 tablespoon on each of 6 dessert plates. Stand the pears on the platter or plates and drizzle 1 tablespoon of the sauce on each pear. Garnish with the mint. Pass any remaining sauce in a small pitcher.

YIELD: 6 servings of 1 pear with about 2 tablespoons of sauce each

COOK'S NOTE: Other cranberry-juice combinations can be substituted for the cranberry-apple. Other frozen berries can be substituted for the raspberries. To produce a clearer sauce and eliminate the seeds, force the raspberry mixture through a fine sieve into a bowl. The sauce provides 8 servings of 2 tablespoons each.

Nutritional Information Per Serving

Calories 125 | Carbohydrate 38 g. | Fat 1 g. | Protein 1 g. | Fiber 5 g.

Nutritional Information Per Serving of Sauce

Calories 20 | Carbohydrate 5 g. | Fat 0 g. | Protein 0 g. | Fiber 0 g.

Fresh Fruit Parfait

Try this refreshing dessert when fresh berries are in season. It also works well at breakfast.

1½ cups yogurt cheese
2 tablespoons honey
½ teaspoon vanilla extract
1 cup sliced fresh strawberries plus
   4 whole, perfect strawberries

1 cup fresh blueberries
1 cup fresh raspberries
4 teaspoons low-fat granola

1. In a mixing bowl, combine the yogurt cheese, honey, and vanilla extract. Beat with an electric mixer until fluffy and smooth.

2. Divide the strawberries among 4 dessert dishes or parfait glasses and top each with 3 tablespoons of the yogurt mixture. Divide the blueberries among the dishes and top each with 3 tablespoons of the yogurt mixture. Divide the raspberries among the dishes and top each with the remaining yogurt mixture. Garnish each parfait with 1 teaspoon of the granola and 1 whole strawberry.

YIELD: 4 servings

Nutritional Information Per Serving

Calories 170 | Carbohydrate 32 g. | Fat 0 g. | Protein 11 g. | Fiber 4 g.

For a 170-calorie dessert

TRADITIONAL	How we lowered calorie density	VOLUMETRICS
Strawberry mousse	▸ Used plenty of fresh berries ▸ Substituted yogurt cheese for cream	Fresh Fruit Parfait

Yogurt Cheese

3 cups nonfat plain yogurt

1. Set a fine-mesh sieve or colander over a bowl. Line it with a double layer of cheesecloth. Spoon in the yogurt and cover the bowl with plastic wrap. Refrigerate for at least 8 hours or overnight. Transfer the yogurt cheese to a covered storage container and discard the liquid.

YIELD: 16 servings of 1 tablespoon each, about 1 cup total

COOK'S NOTE: The yogurt cheese will keep in the refrigerator for up to 1 week. You can vary the flavor by adding fresh chopped herbs, minced garlic, and/or lemon zest. Begin with small amounts, adjusting to taste. One tablespoon counts as a free food.

Nutritional Information Per Serving

Calories 15 | Carbohydrate 2 g. | Fat 0 g. | Protein 2 g. | Fiber 0 g.

Grilled Banana Splits

These make a great ending to a summer evening of grilling.

4 ripe bananas, about ½ pound each
2 tablespoons chocolate chips

½ cup nonfat, frozen vanilla yogurt
4 teaspoons chopped walnuts

1. Preheat a grill or preheat the oven to 400 degrees.

2. Place each banana on its side on a piece of foil. Cut a slit lengthwise across the top. Leave the skin attached.

3. Push ½ tablespoon chocolate chips into the slit of each banana.

4. Wrap the bananas with the foil, leaving the top open. Grill or bake about 15 minutes, or until the chocolate melts.

5. Loosen the foil and press the bananas open a little.

6. Top each banana with 2 tablespoons of the frozen yogurt and sprinkle with 1 teaspoon walnuts.

YIELD: 4 servings

Nutritional Information Per Serving

Calories 185 | Carbohydrate 36 g. | Fat 4 g. | Protein 3 g. | Fiber 3 g.

Raspberry-Apple Crumble

This updated version of an old favorite uses less butter-filled crumb topping, giving this dessert a lower calorie density. Raspberry preserves give it additional flavor.

*4 medium, tart apples, such as Granny
  Smith*
¼ cup orange juice
2 tablespoons raspberry preserves
2 tablespoons quick-cooking oats
2 tablespoons all-purpose flour

2 tablespoons brown sugar
2 tablespoons wheat germ
½ teaspoon ground cinnamon
Pinch salt
1 tablespoon melted butter

1. Preheat the oven to 350 degrees.

2. Peel, core, and thinly slice the apples.

3. Combine the sliced apples, juice, preserves, and ¼ cup water in a bowl. Pour the mixture into an 8-by-8-inch glass baking dish and set aside.

4. Combine the oats, flour, sugar, wheat germ, cinnamon, and salt. Add the melted butter and mix well.

5. Top the apple mixture with the oats mixture, cover, and bake 1 hour, or until the apples are tender. Uncover the dish for the last 10 minutes of baking.

YIELD: 4 servings of 1 cup each

COOK'S NOTE: Other preserve flavors can be used, such as strawberry or blackberry.

Nutritional Information Per Serving

Calories 175 | Carbohydrate 37 g. | Fat 4 g. | Protein 1 g. | Fiber 3 g.

Recipe Index

Recipe Food Groups

RECIPE	MEAT	STARCH	VEGETABLE	FAT	FRUIT	MILK
BREAKFASTS						
Jennifer's Fruit-Smothered Whole-Wheat Buttermilk Pancakes		2		1	1	
Piquant Frittata	2		2	1		
Creamy Apricot Oatmeal		1 ½			1	1
Blueberry Applesauce Muffin		1 ½				
APPETIZERS						
Vegetable Party Platter		1	2	1		⅓
House Dressing						⅓
Mel's Fresh Lemon Hummus		1				
Tex-Mex Salsa		1				
White Bean Bruschetta (2 servings)		1 ½				
Stuffed Mushrooms Florentine			1	1		
SOUPS						
Autumn Harvest Pumpkin Soup		2				
Creamy Broccoli Soup		½	1	1		½
Rustic Tomato Soup			3	1		
Vegetarian Barley Soup		1	2			
Minestrone		1	2			
Hearty Chicken and Vegetable Soup	3	1	2	1		
SANDWICHES						
Almond Chicken Salad Sandwich	2	2		1		
Buffalo Chicken Wraps	3	2	1	1		
Zesty Tuna Salad Pita	3	2		1		
Mediterranean Turkey Sandwich	2	2	1	1		
Open-Faced Roast Beef Sandwich	2	1	1			

RECIPE	MEAT	STARCH	VEGETABLE	FAT	FRUIT	MILK
Salads and Dressings						
Charlie's Greek Salad			1	1		
Volumetrics Salad			3			
Italian Dressing				1		
Tuna and White Bean Salad	3	1	1			
Insalata Mista			1	1		
Fennel, Orange, and Arugula Salad			1	1	½	
SIDES						
Minted Broccoli			1			
Garlic-Roasted Vegetables		½	2			
Stir-Fried Green Beans			2			
MEATLESS						
Bulgar and Vegetable Stuffed Peppers	½	1	2			
Charlie's Pasta Primavera	½	2 ½	3	1		
Veggie-Stuffed Macaroni and Cheese	2 ½	2	1			
Garden-Fresh Vegetable Pizza	1	2	1	1		
BEEF						
Old World Goulash	3	1 ½	2			
Garden Chili	3	1	2	1		
Santa Fe Steak Salad with Lime-Cilantro Dressing	4	1	3	1		
FISH AND SHELLFISH						
Baked Tilapia with Sauteed Vegetables	2 ½		2			
Shrimp Fried Rice	2 ½	2	1	1		
Fillet of Sole and Vegetable Parcels	3 ½		2			
Poach-Roast Salmon with Yogurt and Dill Sauce	3 ½					

Recipe Food Groups

(continued)

RECIPE	MEAT	STARCH	VEGETABLE	FAT	FRUIT	MILK
POULTRY						
Chicken Merlot	3		2			
South of the Border Chicken Stew	3 ½	1	2			
Chicken Provençal	2 ½		1	1		
Stir-Fried Turkey with Crunchy Vegetables	3	1	3			
DESSERTS						
Balsamic Berries					1	
Ruby-Red Poached Pears with Raspberry Sauce					2	
Fresh Fruit Parfait					1	1
Grilled Banana Splits		1		1	1	
Raspberry-Apple Crumble		1 ½			1	